# HOME LIFE BOOK FOUR

Alice Thomas Ellis was born in Liverpool and educated at Bangor Grammar School and Liverpool School of Art. She is the author of eight widely praised novels, *The Sin Eater*, *The Birds of the Air*, *The 27th Kingdom*, *The Other Side of the Fire*, *Unexplained Laughter*, *The Skeleton in the Cupboard*, *The Clothes in the Wardrobe* and *The Fly in the Ointment*, and two studies of juvenile delinquency, *Secrets of Strangers* and *The Loss of the Good Authority*, written with a psychiatrist, Tom Pitt-Aikens. In 1985 she started writing a weekly column in the *Spectator* under the title 'Home Life', which she continued until the end of 1989, and which gained her a readership even wider than her novels. She lives in London and Wales with her husband and five children.

# Home Life
## Book Four

Alice Thomas Ellis

with illustrations by Zé

FLAMINGO
Published by Fontana Paperbacks

First published by Gerald Duckworth & Co. Ltd, 1989
This Flamingo edition first published
in 1990 by Fontana Paperbacks

Flamingo is an imprint of
Fontana Paperbacks, part of
Harper Collins Publishers,
8 Grafton Street, London W1X 3LA

The text of this book appeared originally
as articles in the *Spectator*

Printed and bound in Great Britain by
Collins, Glasgow

# Contents

## January

| | |
|---|---|
| Know thyself | 9 |
| January sails | 12 |
| Pet worries | 14 |
| Weather moan | 17 |

## February

| | |
|---|---|
| Ill-judged | 22 |
| All in the mind | 24 |
| Colour problem | 27 |
| Night owls | 30 |

## March

| | |
|---|---|
| Fear of flying | 34 |
| Tale of the unexpected | 36 |
| Why, oh why? | 39 |
| Motorway madness | 43 |

## April

| | |
|---|---|
| Huffing and puffing | 48 |
| Don't take it with you | 51 |
| At the crossroads | 54 |
| Buffet garni | 57 |

## May

| | |
|---|---|
| Murder most tasteful | 62 |
| Looking on the bright side | 64 |
| There be dragons | 67 |
| A ripping good day | 70 |

## June

| | |
|---|---|
| Vital statistics | 76 |
| A sparrow falls | 78 |
| Table talk | 81 |
| Whose toothbrush? | 85 |

## July

| | |
|---|---|
| I remember it well | 90 |
| Sixties' child | 92 |
| Crumbling urns | 95 |
| Enchanting Welshmen | 98 |

## August

| | |
|---|---|
| Six legs bad | 104 |
| Plumbing the depths | 106 |
| Frites with everything | 109 |
| French polish | 112 |

## September

| | |
|---|---|
| Hotel du lack | 118 |
| Fundamental error | 120 |
| A dusty answer | 124 |
| Not so funny | 126 |

## October

| | |
|---|---|
| Escape route | 132 |
| Designs on the young | 134 |
| Sheep shock | 137 |
| Hawkers welcome | 140 |

## November

| | |
|---|---|
| Glastonbury tour | 146 |
| Wall to wall | 149 |
| Open-mouthed | 151 |
| Strong medicine | 154 |

## December

| | |
|---|---|
| Skip ahoy | 160 |
| No strings on me | 162 |
| Nappy Christmas | 164 |
| Funny sort of flu | 167 |

# January

# Know thyself

I have always felt that the wise person as she floats through life on her broomstick should utilise the brushing end to obscure any footprints she may have left behind her. She should burn her letters, put misleading captions on her photographs and, when necessary, tell whoppers. This is because the biographical industry is expanding in rather the same way as the 'service' industries, tourism and entertainment. There are people everywhere prepared to write about other people, just as there are people everywhere prepared to take up hamburger franchises and go round with the smell of boiling oil in their hair. And this is because computers are doing everything else – all the sums and flying the aeroplanes. Bored and underemployed, humankind has to discover other means of passing the time and Satan always finds work for idle hands. Anyone who has ever had so much as a squeak written about him in the public presses will know that inaccuracies will have crept in (this is the usual way of putting it: it implies that the journalist is blameless and that these little errors have slithered, ratlike, down the ropes and cables of passing ships to despoil the text). They ascribe foreign sentiments to you and put extraordinary words in your mouth; they get your age wrong – or even worse, right – and they scour the land for the most execrable photograph of you that has ever been taken. 'They have a living to earn,' you say to yourself resignedly. You remind yourself that tomorrow's mass murder or natural disaster will expunge the memory of yesterday's scurrilous paragraph, and, if you're in the trade, you promptly take up your pen and do the same thing to some other innocent. The trouble is that while it is annoying to be misunderstood it is intolerble to be fully exposed: a truly no-win situation, unless you elect to keep your mouth shut and your head so far below the parapet you're down in the dungeons.

I am thinking on these lines because it has been suggested that I should write an autobiography, and as I've done very little out of the ordinary there isn't very much to say. Here is the dilemma. Either I do it myself and bore the pants off people, or I don't and face the possibility that when I'm dead some postgraduate student with time on her hands will take the meagre facts and make something more diverting out of them. A chilling prospect. Biographers when thwarted by a barren patch in the life of their subjects frequently indulge in the wildest speculation: 'What was in Araminta's thoughts as she gazed out across the tossing waves, her blue eyes thoughtful...' or 'her grey eyes grave', or 'one of her eyes black'. As often as not they tell you. Not that our everyday life is uneventful. On the contrary I find it rather wearing in its variety, but it is the variety of minor domestic harassment rather than major upheaval. 'The floor fell out of the lavatory' is not altogether lacking in drama, but it doesn't have the same *élan* as 'At this point I shot my third husband and had to flee the country'.

Christmas, for instance, was not boring. Discretion inhibits me yet again from putting all the facts before you and we are back in another dilemma. Having said this I fear that those with the more lurid imaginations will be picturing scenes of nameless vice and debauchery, whereas the family members all behaved with commendable decorum. It is the friends who usually add that touch of spice, the *je ne sais quoi* to these occasions: finding them tucked up in the nutshells as Boxing Day dawns, or learning that they had whiled away the grey hours after picking the turkey bones by painting pictures not of, but *on*, each other. What I'd really like to do is write biographies of my friends capering in the sunlight while I sit in the shade with my parasol and sun-glasses, sipping something long and cool – and at the moment – non-alcoholic. I watched the TV programme about our Home Life through the bottom of a whisky glass and consequently was left with a blurred impression of wellies splashing through puddles and owls hooting. I remember that Remi Adefarisin's photography was beautiful, and Nadia Hagger is a genius to bring order to all of us tripping over each other, but I've forgotten the rest. This is another problem with autobiography. I've forgotten almost everything and my recollections often differ from those of other people. The mite in my unconscious came up with another put-down the other morning. He said: 'What's more – you're Alias Thomas Somebody Else'. You can't write an autobiography when you don't know who you are.

# January sails

I'm all at sea. Well, not precisely sea. To be perfectly honest, I haven't got much idea where I am. I think we started from Gosport and we're going to the Isle of Wight, but we've been back and forth across stretches of water quite a lot and I'm losing count. It reminds me of the time we went on a joy ride across the Suez Canal. I got parted from the third son and whisked off by a couple of veiled ladies in a motor car and we passed each other frequently going from Port Said to the other side and back. I didn't really mind. I like boats.

This boat has what I think are described as 'possibilities'. It's about the same size as our Cortina but deeper – I can just stand upright in it, although I've clouted myself on the head standing up suddenly in a shorter bit, and there must be more of it under the water, although there's also quite a bit of water in it. Never mind: I've got plastic trousers on and I'm sitting on somebody's anorak. Every now and then I hear shouted instructions to turn left at the cormorant on the red pole, which doesn't square with what I remember of C.S. Forester but makes more sense. The engine is now working again, and so it doesn't matter so much that there seems to be no wind around to get in the sails. There are three men out there picking bits of things up and tying them to other bits of things.

My friend the analyst occasionally picks things up and

12

wonders aloud what they're for. He is steering the boat perfectly beautifully and says that if the springboard, or sprung plank or whatever it is, holds out we should make it to shore before nightfall – especially since one of the chaps out there, one Keith, is a geographer by trade. I find that reassuring, since the coastline has an inchoate air, and if it was me driving I should simply aim for all of it. It is nice to be with people who can choose a specific part and actually (I trust) end up there. John was perfectly brilliant restarting the engine while Keith pulled on a bit of string, and my admiration for them all is unbounded. I should have been dismayed if we'd had to float around all night in the cold and damp waiting for the hurricanes to start up again.

We spent last night in great, if miniature, comfort on John's boat, which is all shiny and warm and watertight and has a cupboard for whisky. I wondered if this way of life might not be what I've been looking for, but we have just passed a rather nice castle which Queen Victoria once had her eye on (the owner wouldn't sell it) and I am reminded that it is quite pleasant to be able to swing a cat if you feel so inclined. My friend the analyst is given to swinging his cat (he says it likes it) and if he keeps up the practice in this boat he'll bash its brains out.

Perhaps the ideal is to live in more spacious accommodation and simply to take to sea when you feel like fish for tea or you've had a row with the neighbours. It was certainly very peaceful when the engine cut out. Not a sound for miles around, although that could have changed if it hadn't started again. Horrid oaths and shrieks of 'Another fine mess you've got me into'. However, we're almost there now, and then all we have to do is leap on the ferry and go back the way we came. The point is: this boat is being taken ashore so that John can mend it, and until now it was on the wrong – the other – shore. I really must sit down with a map of the Solent and relevant areas and try and work out exactly where I've been, and how often. Not that it really matters. The sea breeze in January is most refreshing.

I had a frozen shoulder and now I don't care as much because the rest of me is frozen too.

# Pet worries

A note came through the door the other day to tell us that a small cat from further up the road was missing, and asking us to look out for it. 'Missing' is an awful word, rather worse than 'dead'. There have been many such notices over the years posted on garden gates and lamp posts and they have all served to increase my innate pessimism and deep mistrust of certain sections of the human race – glove-, muff- and tippet-makers for a start. I read only recently that the fashion for the Russian look has resulted in a fall in the incidence of black cats who then appear in a new guise – as collars round the necks of the *beau monde*, or whoever it is these days who keeps up with the fashion. (In Camden Town it seems to be every woman for herself, and none of us is likely to appear in *Vogue*.)

That's beside the point. Anthony Grayling told me that there are already remarkably few *pure* black cats in England because our ancestors suspected them of consorting with witches and burned them and drowned

*Pet worries*

them and stoned them. Both our cats are black, but
Cadders has a white bib, and if you grab Puss, who is at
first sight as black as your hat, and peer under her chin
there will be seen a small white spot. I don't suppose these
tiny flaws would be enough to deter the determined
accessory-maker and I contemplated rubbing chewing
gum into their fur, or dusting them with Harpic to take
the shine out. On further reflection and closer inspection I
decided it probably wasn't necessary since both are
unashamed moggies and their coats could never be
mistaken for mink. Then I remembered a Chinese
take-away of some years ago, and a chicken with very
unusual vertebrae for its species. We studied these bones
for some time, surmising, before we threw them away.
Nobody said much but we never returned to that
particular restaurant. They eat dogs too in some parts of
the world, *and* guinea pigs.

The third son found a lost dog the other day – or rather
the dog found us. I was flying round in a panic because the
daughter was – not lost, but late: an hour late, which in my
book is much the same as lost. I had left the gate and the
bottom door open while I dithered on the corner,
wringing my hands and peering to left and right, and the
dog strolled into the house wearing the confident and
pleased expression of an invited guest expecting a good
time. Part of my panic was due to the fact that a car was
waiting to take us off to an appointment, so when the
daughter finally appeared (she'd got a few wrong buses)
we shot off without further delay. When we got back I
asked what had happened to the dog – a golden labrador,
as it happens – and a thrilling tale unfolded. It had had a
collar with the name of its owner on it, a reverend
gentleman. So the son very sensibly went round to the
church for further details and then telephoned the good

Father, who was very startled to hear that his pet was at large, as it was supposed to be staying with friends in the district. He gave the son the address, and the son, with the dog in tow on a pair of braces or a belt or something, went round to check it out. The door to the flat was smashed open and household effects were strewn all over the place. The burglar had been, and the dog had taken the opportunity to slip out for a walk. I know there's a moral somewhere in all this, but at the moment it escapes me.

Man of God          Dog of Man of God

# Weather moan

There is something odd about the weather. Perhaps there always is, but recently it's been becoming more obvious and affecting the population more noticeably. The birds have been busily tweaking twigs off the tree outside the bedroom window when they should still be recovering from Christmas, huddled up in the barn with their heads under their wings and waiting for their human neighbours to break the ice on the puddles so they can have a drink. At least they don't have to bother about what to wear. When it gets nippy they just need to fluff out their feathers a bit, whereas the human neighbours have to apply thought to the problem. I keep seeing ladies doggedly attired in big fur hats and boots because they bought them to be fashionable in a wintry sort of way and that's what they're damn well going to do. Their little faces, which are meant to look pale and flowerlike under their Anna Karenina hats (necks like slender stalks), go all red and sweaty in the unseasonal warmth.

Janet gets up early, looks out at the grey sky, piles on a few sweaters and spends the rest of the day peeling them off like an onion. I got up this morning, contemplated the tweeds, thought 'The hell with it' and put on an Indian cotton. It makes me uneasy. It makes me cross too because one cannot plan where to go any more than what to wear. Beryl and I were about to leave for the country to do some work in peace when the weather-man announced that there was ice and snow down there, and conditions were treacherous. Well, they may be; but it's hard to believe, when the shrubs round here are shaking out their spring apparel and I can walk into the backyard in my nightdress to feed the cats. I think the weather-man has lost his nerve after failing to predict the hurricane and is determined to hedge his bets. Janet was listening to him the other day and he forecast just about everything – some sun, some showers, frost, snow, thunderstorms and high winds. Apart from an earthquake and temperatures in the eighties that's about it. What is a person to do apart from stay indoors with several changes of attire laid judiciously to hand? There are few things worse than going out to dine in your heavy velvet with people who haven't noticed that spring is a little early this year and have the central heating going at full blast. It is worse than dining with Scots who don't have central heating at all. You can always put your coat on or borrow a plaid, while it is not permissible to strip down to your knickers and vest. These unexpectedly clement but dreary climatic conditions serve to unsettle us and muddle our view of the universe.

Marks & Spencers don't help. I still have three quarters of a Christmas cake left and they've got hot-cross buns on their shelves, for God's sake. *Lent* hasn't even started yet. Has it? I'm getting disoriented with the almond blossom tossing about over the road and pictures of David Steel on telly somewhere up north with snowflakes drifting round him. Now the gales seem to be starting up again and I hear they've had snow in Finchley. I keep opening the window to see if I've gone mad and it's really below freezing out there, but it isn't. It gives me the same sort of feeling as going to sleep in the afternoon and waking up not knowing whether it's morning or midnight. I feel sorry for the dormice. It must be perfectly ghastly to wake from hibernation and not know whether it's December or May and whether you've missed out on the hot-cross buns. We must all give up on the aerosol deodorants before we melt the ice-cap and find ourselves in real trouble.

# February

# Ill-judged

I don't like judges much. I haven't met many socially, because they mix only with each other, and I assure you I have not yet met one in his official capacity; but I do know that elevation to the judiciary tends to make men mad.

We had one living near us once. One day the Queen made him a Knight as well as a judge and the next day a little boy knocked on his door (as he did most days) to ask if *his* little boy could come out and play. The judge said, 'Wait here a moment, little boy, and I'll ask Lady...' he meant his wife. Oh God. On another occasion his next-door neighbour, attempting to cross the road from A to B in the vicinity of the Law Courts, had the galling experience of being stopped by a policeman halting all traffic so that the judge could sail across the road *en grande tenue* with *such* an expression of superlative smugness that the neighbour longed only to jump up and down on his wig.

I have known other men who were turned into Knights, and some who were made Lords, and after a certain initial bout of swank (signified in the first place by a change in their writing paper – improved quality and embossed headings – and a tendency to send more letters to people than is usual) they have settled down and eaten the crusts on their bacon sandwiches much like the rest of us. It is being made a judge that goes straight to the head and addles the brains. The stories I could tell you – only I can't because writs for contempt of court, the Official Secrets Act, D Notices, men in dark coats and Lord knows what else would come winging round my ears like wasps. Sickening. My cousin was something in the Lord Chancellor's office once, but he kept coming across judges so he went off and lived abroad. He couldn't stand it. The thing is – judges don't see things like the rest of us. Evidence which to you and me and the binman is incontrovertible is dismissed by judges as irrelevant. 'I have made up my mind, now kindly don't confuse me with the facts' is a statement arising from possibly the most infuriating attitude known to mankind. When people who lay claim to logical processes of thought, unbiased methods of investigation and impartial analysis appear to be a bunch of fat-headed chumps it worries the populace. We suspect that it is even worse than it seems, since, by the law of averages, they can't all be total bone from the neck up, and we catch a strong whiff of *Rattus Rattus* scampering through the corridors of power. Even a pinch of political expediency dropped into the judicial process makes a nasty simmering brew, and sooner or later something will go off bang. I have frequently been told by smooth-faced gentlemen in positions of influence not to worry my little head about it (and if I ever do come up before a judge I shall be arraigned on a charge of murdering one of them) and to leave these matters to the experts. Well, it would be nice if we could, but on the evidence we would be most ill-advised to do so. Experts all over the place – not only judges, but politicians, scientists, town-planners, etc. – are manifestly nuts. If you take your eyes off them for a second they conspire to erect a nuclear shopping precinct with a landscaped conifer plantation on your village green, and tax you to pay for it. Keeping your wary, weary eyes on them is as exhaustingly tiresome as being a passenger on a plane and having to go by the minute to check that the pilot isn't drunk and the co-pilot isn't distracted by the air-hostess's ankles. Not being able to trust those who are supposed to be in charge is a waste of all our time, and the possibility that some people in positions of power are clinically insane is not reassuring. The psychopath is incapable of realising that there are some of us out there who are not prepared to share in his delusion. He fondly believes that his need to control without question will be gratified simply because it is so urgent to him. What's more he insists that he does what he does for our own good (in the national interest). This is called paranoia, stems from the madman's need to identify himself with the universe and calls for immediate treatment. Unfortunately, the madman does not understand that he is cuckoo, so all is lost. All one can say is 'Judge not that ye be not judged, and if you must, *do* try and get it right, or, when you come up before the Great Tribunal, God will be cross.'

# All in the mind

I was talking to an afflicted friend on the telephone the other day and as I concluded the conversation and turned away I said compassionately that he had had yet another breakdown. I assumed a pitiful expression and was in

mid-sigh when Janet remarked acidly that she hoped he'd sent for the AA then. She has very little patience with people exhibiting signs of the vapours, or a general inability to cope with the vicissitudes of life. 'Pull yourself together,' she says; which are the last words you hear, as my friend Rex once observed, as you hurtle into the depths of the mental ward.

In view of this it is unfortunate that she has developed symptoms of what I believe is known as the Royal Free virus. These symptoms are evident to no one but the sufferer and were disregarded by the medical profession until a number of them contracted it and were forced to agree that it did indeed exist and was debilitating in its effects. She has to keep sitting down. I think I've probably had it always. Luckily she seems to be getting better now. I had visions of us pushing Nanny round in a bath-chair until the end of all our days. In the meantime she's knocked the handles off about half a dozen jugs. They sit, these poor amputees, on the shelf awaiting medical attention. I bought some super-glue to mend them but my friend the analyst posted it. He was walking along, doubtless pondering the complexities of the Oedipal situation, clutching a letter, and the super-glue in a paper bag, and when he got home he found he still had the letter. I put a note in the box for the postman asking him to return the super-glue to the Institute of Psychoanalysis. I don't know what the GPO will make of it.

There's a lot of madness around, of one sort and another. Extreme carelessness is, in my opinion, a type of insanity, and I keep losing things. A red purse, a brand-new brooch that I hadn't even worn, the dry mustard, two pairs of warm tights, and a scarf of many colours. I never wear the scarf, but now I've lost it I want it. I waste hours looking hopelessly in places I've already searched. There was some money in the purse too, but now money has so largely lost its value it doesn't seem to matter all that much. It was only a few quid. What could have been more serious was the absent-mindedness of the Inland Revenue who sent four identical tax demands on four consecutive days. If I was stupid I might have paid all of them – stupid and rich, that is. Perhaps their computer has the new computer virus that muddles up the system and wipes their memories clean. Perhaps we've all got it. Certainly many of my friends have an increasing tendency to repeat themselves, showing no signs of remembering that they've told that story before – several times before – and the children consistently forget that I've lent them a fiver twice that week already. Theories as to the cause of all this aberration vary widely – from advancing age, which can't be so in the case of the youngest child – to the changing weather (due to a combination of felled rainforest and the effect of fast-food containers on the atmosphere) and the influence of malign aliens.

Deirdre inclines to the latter explanation. Like the rest of us she fondly believed that if beings from space were amongst us it was because their intentions were benevolent and they wished to show us how to comport ourselves with dignity. Then she saw a programme featuring a lady who, driving along in Australia, had been cut up by a flying saucer. As Deirdre remarked indignantly, we've got enough of that sort of thing without Martians coming along to add their whack. How worrying if, like gods, they know that those whom they wish to destroy they must first make mad. Nothing makes people madder than being cut up on the motorway. Half of us believe in UFOs, half of us don't and each faction believes the other to be deluded. Happily Janet shares my views on this, but next time I feel a trauma coming on and she tells me to get a grip on myself I shall tell her her virus is all in the mind.

# Colour problem

Seated between Tom Wolfe and David Frost at a very pleasant dinner the other evening, I found myself cheerfully refusing the vino in order to savour more completely the felicities of the situation arranged by our perfect hostess, Drue Heinz, and the interesting conversation. I very seldom go out in Society after dark because after dark is bedtime; I am not, by nature, gregarious, and I usually find myself sandwiched between people who wish only to argue with each other about the merits of some musical performance. In this case, in the absence of chloroform, I morosely sink all that is put before me, even reaching out for the claret, than which I would actually rather drink Syrup of Figs. It was most invigorating to enjoy an evening out. And I met P.J. Kavanagh whom I hadn't seen since he was a little boy at his school in Wales. I used to pass him in the mornings on the way to my own school. He never saw me – probably, we agreed, because I was always engulfed in a horrible school hat, chewing the chin elastic. I did have a nice time – at the party, that is, not on the way to school. (It was probably school that set me on the road to being a recluse, since you can't get away from your fellows in a classroom any more than you can at a dinner party.)

Teeny little coincidences kept coming up during the evening. For instance when I was at school my house colour was mauve which is probably why I have never much cared for this shade. Tom Wolfe said he had planned to write a book with a long title containing the word *mauve*, only no one ever knew how to pronounce it – *morv* or *mohv*. It's in the same category as *scon*, *scohn* or *scoon* and *varz*, *vaze* and *vorz*: you pays your money and you takes your choice. I recently bought a mauve blouse because spring is coming. I have a new black coat and skirt, and when I was a girl in Liverpool I always greeted the onset of spring in a black coat and skirt with a bunch of violets pinned to it. The mauve blouse, I thought, would go nicely with the bunch of violets, except that now, as I soon realised, you can't get bunches of violets any more and, if you can, they don't smell of anything, let alone violets, and they drop dead as soon as you look at them. So there I am with an expensive new blouse in a colour I don't like with a name I can't pronounce. I try thinking of it as lilac, or lavender, or even pale purple, but it stays mauve. I had a frock once which I tried to think of as dark red, but it was puce: it stubbornly remained puce, and in the end I had to throw it away. Puce is the colour of people having apoplexy, and mauve (pronounce it how you like) is the colour of people who've died. Of all the colours in the spectrum red and blue make the unhappiest mix. Even porphyria is an illness, and I don't know why we persevere in trying to regard purple as becoming to the complexion.

I was about to speak of this to my neighbour when I remembered a story told by my friend Laura. Her father was a minister in Scotland, and one day a parishioner's baby died. He went to visit the family and was disconcerted to find the coffin open. On enquiring why they hadn't nailed it down he was told it was because the wee bairn was such a pretty shade of blue. I think this 'blue' is what I would describe as mauve, and it doesn't encourage me to regard my blouse with any greater favour.

Happily at this point the conversation turned to writing methods and I vowed to mend my ways in this respect before I turn blue – or whatever – myself. If I methodically take S. Maugham's advice and apply the seat of the pants to the seat of the chair I might feel justified in going about more in the evenings, thereby acquiring food for thought. I shall never like that purple muck they squash out of grapes, but if the company's amusing who needs it?

# Night owls

I was not up with the lark this morning because I was up all night with a positive parliament of fowls. We went to bed late, since we were watching John Mills being quietly staunch in the face of disaster and Richard Attenborough turning from a bit of a mess of a seaman second-class into a real brick – or, as they put it in the accents of the 40s, a jolly good chep. They went down with their sub: right down to the bottom of the ocean, where they sat heroically eating corned beef with a knife and fork off a plate while the air ran out.

It was the funniest film we'd seen in years. 'Send up an oil slick so the salvage team can see were you are,' we cried. 'I say sir', suggested a rating humbly, 'should we send up an oil slick so the salvage team can see where we are?' 'My word, what a whizz of an idea' (or words to that effect) cried John Mills, clapping a hand to his forehead. In the end there were four of them left down there until one died – oddly enough, it seems of malaria – and then there were three. They played cards while they waited. We waited too, confidently expecting them to be rescued, but no: a force 10 blew up on the surface, so the salvage team went home to the pub and John Mills put aside his corned beef to read aloud from the prayer book.

It was rather moving, but also terribly annoying, so I went to bed and lay awake planning a more satisfactory ending. I had just introduced Jaws to bite off the conning tower when a bird started tweeting in the tree next door. It was about 2 am and a bit early for the dawn chorus, but the weather was mild and the street lighting on, so I concluded it was just confused; or perhaps it was being bothered by a cat creeping up its tree. I put it out of my mind while I wrote in a part for Jean Simmons, or possibly Margaret Lockwood. One of them might have stowed away for'ard and her husband (I saw him as James Mason or Stewart Grainger) would be the captain of the rescue ship and have a hunch she was down there. The actual captain of the rescue ship was lamentably defeatist, having no real incentive to continue the salvage exercise. A little bit of wind and he cut the cables and floated off. If they'd made that film some years later Henry Fonda would have gone down and got them out single-handed.

Thus musing and unable to sleep, I next heard a screech owl screeching. This is not unusual in our road, and it is appropriate for owls to express themselves in this fashion at two in the morning, so I didn't mind, but then simultaneously I heard a *kraak* as of a raven croaking. We have ravens on the hill behind us in the country, but in London I believe they're all confined to the Tower. I don't know when I last saw a crow locally, although a jay occasionally flies past, but we do have two magpies who go to great pains never to be seen together. Presumably they are each married to other magpies. They make the unmusical noise common to the crow family, and I imagine the spouse of one of them had just discovered what was going on. Richard Attenborough had trouble with his wife in the submarine film. She was always going dancing, and squandering the extra half crown he got for spending so much time under the water.

The church clock struck three and these ill-assorted

birds were still variously tweeting, shrieking and croaking whenever a thought occurred to them. In the magpie altercation there was a distinct note of '...and what's *more*'. Then they woke a little dog up the road. Why do little dogs bark so much more than big ones? I waited fatalistically for a burglar alarm to go off but I must have gone to sleep – goodness knows how, because the next sound I heard was *all* the little birds tweeting, and a seagull crying. There are thousands of them round here because they don't bother ever going to sea any more, and I don't blame them, when you think of the conditions. I still feel discontented when I think of J. Mills, R. Attenborough and the other chep sitting playing cards with the malaria victim laid out on a bunk and the duffel-coated toff on top leaving them to their fate. They took it remarkably well, I must say. I suppose it was, at least, very quiet down there. No dawn chorus.

# March

# Fear of flying

Alfie says he likes the element of risk in flying. He finds it exciting. I don't. The element of risk in flying is one of the things I like least about it. People keep telling me it's the safest means of transport. But not if you're on the same flight path as another aeroplane coming from the opposite direction it isn't. Not a bit. If you're in a car and some fool comes hurtling towards you you can attempt evasive action, and if that fails you stand a chance of rolling out on to *terra firma*. You can't get out of a dodgy aeroplane and walk. This simple, self-evident truth is what disinclines me from getting into one. I was interested to learn that a recent near-miss involved a Bulgarian aeroplane since I was in the back of one of them once. It rattled all the way to Sofia but the most startling thing about it was the food – I use the term loosely – which I have never quite found words to describe. At its simplest it comprised a dark-brown slab of cold meat, grained and textured rather like sodden pine wood, a perfectly *enormous* tomato, a hunk of bread of the consistency of dry pine wood, and a tasteful *mélange* of cold rice and cold chips. Happily I was too terrified to be hungry, but I did try the butter. Bulgarian butter, I can tell you, is something else again. If I say it tastes more of sick than anything you may get some slight idea.

## Fear of flying

I heard a particularly alarming tale the other day from a young photographer. She had a friend who was flying along in an aeroplane when the pilot put the thing on automatic and went off to the loo. The co-pilot emerged to chat up the stewardess, and the navigator came out for a stroll up the aisle, when suddenly, wallop – the plane hit an air-pocket and fell about 4,000 feet. All the luggage leapt out of the racks, the passengers were flung about, the pilot was concussed in the loo, and the anti-terrorist device activated itself, thereby isolating the flight deck. There followed a spirited interlude with passengers and crew wildly hacking at the safety doors in order to get at the controls. Now, that wouldn't happen in a Cortina Estate. Nor does a trip in the car involve imprisonment in an airport lounge, where the disaffected are likely to shoot at you.

I think of this because one of those creepy coincidences has just crept up on me. A delightful young woman called in order to persuade Someone and me to fly to Geneva to talk to her literary society. I said I was averse to everything pertaining to flying and could we take the train, and she said a friend of her sister's had been killed in the Athens airport shoot-out of some years ago and she herself had been a passenger in one of the planes involved in the most recent near-miss. Not too amazing a coincidence, you would think, but wait. The telephone rang (this was about an hour after I'd moaned about Bulgarian aeroplanes) and it was Isobel from next door to say she'd just returned from Russia (I don't know why the young feel it necessary to ring from next door: they wouldn't have to fly to get round here) and the food had been inedible, and the next plane out after hers had just crashed. I immediately had a sense of responsibility which I put aside in favour of the rather less disagreeable feeling that I merely had some

35

sort of second sight. Then the phone rang again and it was the fourth son speaking from LA. He is the only member of the family actually to fly aeroplanes himself. Last summer his brother dreamed that he had crashed and I made him telephone immediately to dissuade our pilot from taking off in the near future. What happened next was that the dreaming brother had three ribs broken in a car accident while on holiday with my favourite Logical Positivist. His second sight is slightly out of kilter.

When I was a child by the sea a small aeroplane hit our local mountain and fell on to the shore. We all went to look at the wreckage and there was something rarely, intensely pitiable about it: sadder than a broken car – just as dead birds can seem more dead than dead rabbits, out of their element on the ground.

As somebody remarked only the other day – it isn't the fear of flying that keeps us earthbound. It's the fear of crashing. I've been trying to explain that for years, only nobody ever listens to me. *Listen* to me, Alfie.

# Tale of the unexpected

I was wakened quite late the other morning, or rather afternoon, by an awful little bird sitting on a topmost bough making a noise like an unoiled hinge. Musical it wasn't. He was very small and a bit yellow and I must ask Janet (who knows about these things) what the little horror is called so I can put his name in a drawer.

We were staying in the country for a few days because I had just heard from an editor asking if I had finished the project on which I am engaged. There is nothing like those words for reminding one that one had better make a start, so we shot off to meet Gladys Mary who is helping me with the said project.

We arrived in a blizzard and didn't take our coats off for the first two days while the house gradually warmed up. Then one evening we were just relaxing and thinking about going to bed when the third son and Neil had the sort of experience we could all do without. They were in the barn enjoying an innocent and bracing game of ping-pong when suddenly upon their ears fell the fearful words 'Evenin' all', followed by the sound of size twelves on the barn steps. The ping-pong ball froze in mid-flight, the words 'I never dunnit' hung unuttered on the air and the two of them stared wildly around wondering if there was any evidence they should fling a hasty tarpaulin over. I ask myself if policemen have this effect on families other than our own.

The boys led the officers of the law across to the house where I, in my turn, nearly suffered cardiac arrest, since I always first expect them to tell me that somebody has died. It must be very thankless being a policeman. After the initial shock I found myself surmising shiftily whether I should hide the Scotch behind a chair leg, and whether smoking was illegal in one's own sitting-room. It was reassuring to see one accepting a fag from the son, but I restrained myself from asking ingratiatingly whether they were permitted to drink on duty.

The reason for their unexpected presence was that four teenagers on a Duke of Edinburgh Award Scheme or something had failed to return to base at the correct time and were wandering around somewhere up on the moors.

We left all the lights blazing to guide them down, should they drift our way, and crawled off to bed, where I found I couldn't sleep. Then the ghosts started talking downstairs. Last time I heard them they were all men, but this time I could hear a woman's voice too. I strained my ears to try and distinguish words, but this isn't possible, and anyway they indubitably speak in old Welsh.

Next day Gladys Mary, whose bedroom was just above the room where our phantoms congregate, said she had heard them too. Gladys Mary is quite amazing. She had worked solidly all day on 'my' project while I had spent half the afternoon in exhausted slumber. She had written an article in bed until about 3 am with the ghosts all gassing away downstairs; then she got up at the crack of dawn, hit the ground running and I wouldn't be at all surprised if she'd written a poem before breakfast. What's more she had had a fire at home in her airing cupboard and her golden curls were still full of smoke. *And* she'd driven miles to get to us, traversing the Berwyns in the snow – an unnerving experience necessitating restorative cordials and warm sympathy. I wish I knew where she got her energy.

We heard the helicopter plying to and fro in search of the lost teenagers, but then came the cheerful news that they'd turned up in the pub over on the other side, so I had another nap to celebrate, wondering how many of the ghosts got that way by finding themselves benighted up on the mountain. I was once told by the oldest inhabitant of a previous owner-occupier who rode into the village on his horse and never returned. The horse came back but he was found floating face down in the stream. From the tone of the account I gathered that this had happened yesterday, but it transpired that the granny of the granny of the granny of the oldest inhabitant had told him about it. Time, while not precisely standing still, does tend to lounge around a bit here. There had been a suspicion that the drowned man had not died an accidental death – some talk of sheep rustling and bad feeling – and I wondered who had had the task of enforcing the law in those far off days and whether they had said 'Evenin' all'. Perhaps if I bone up on my Welsh, burnish up my courage and come down one night to join the talking ghosts I shall find out. I am pretty sure that, in view of the impression they made, the shades of our two policemen will continue to alarm generations to come should they chance to be playing ping-pong in the barn as night thickens.

# Why, oh why?

Mysteries, mysteries. Why, wonders the fifth son, does walloping a bottle on the edge of the table enable one to remove its lid, and why does spit make his army boots shine?

Why is there never a policeman around when you want one, and why are there always two on the spot as you draw up on a double yellow line? I ask myself why a perfect stranger imagines I'm about to give him sixty-five quid. This lunatic rang up the other day when I was in exile, working in the Acton flat. He said his principals had elected to give me £6000 and a foreign holiday. Oh yeah? I said. Three questions, he said. Was I over eighteen, would I be at home for the next hour and would I have sixty-five pounds in cash when he sent his messenger round? No, I said. On the other hand he must have been puzzled to hear that I didn't know what my address was. I get taken to the flat, so I don't need to know. Nor do I know what my telephone number there is. It isn't on the hand-set. Still, as the analyst says, you don't need to know your own telephone number unless you want to talk to yourself. In which case you probably stand in need of his treatment.

Alfie and I had a very bewildering time yesterday. He came round to do the cleaning and then he didn't feel like it so he came shopping with me instead. It took us two hours to doddle up and down the High Street – about two hundred yards of it – while I systematically forgot what I wanted. A rich mix of eccentrics roam Camden High Street at the weekend, some of them distinctly disconcerting. Why, I wondered, did that man have a dog in his pocket? Had that girl looked in the mirror before she came out and, if so, why had she not swiftly changed her clothes? How had that man persuaded his hair into the condition of hempen rope, and why had it struck him as a good idea? Who is the Red Indian in the cowboy hat with a meerschaum pipe stuck in his face? What does he have for breakfast? And why has the Post Office carpeted its floor when drunks are not infrequently sick in there and the street outside is already carpeted with dog mess? We passed a small lady tripping – tripping is the only word for it – along, with her head held at a winsome angle and her little finger coquettishly cocked. Alfie said she'd spoken to him once and told him she was the bird of the world. Really? he'd said. Yes, she'd said – she was a bird princess. Then we passed the drop-in centre for the homeless. Alfie said it was amazing in there. They had Roman columns of coffee tins, and piles and piles of *enormous* boxes of condoms. The homeless could pop in in the morning and have bacon and egg for breakfast with fried slices and tomatoes while watching a film on a video screen, and then if they felt like a spot of the other on the way out they could have a free condom as a going-away present. Alfie is a positive mine of information. We forgot to buy butter and cheese in Marks and Spencer; then the lady at the greengrocers' said they did a jolly good Canadian Cheddar in Gateway, so we went there. I hadn't got any money and I had to keep signing cheques, so I said we could buy the wine there too and do it all on one cheque, only we were stuck in a queue and I couldn't get at the drinks counter. I told Alfie to leap the barriers and collar a couple of bottles of Bulgarian, but he said he'd gone all limp and he couldn't. We roared at each other a bit and then staggered to the off-licence. On the way we passed a restaurant with a tree outside stuck in a rather nice earthenware pot. The owners clearly valued this pot because they'd chained the tree to the wall. The sight was too much for Alfie, who went almost terminally limp. All a thief would need to do, he said, was nick the pot from underneath and leave the tree dangling. Cor, stone the crows.

When we got home I wondered why I'd bought a huge lump of celeriac, because it's a bastard to peel – lots of convolutions at the top – and I was much too tired to wrestle with it. You do it, Alfie, I suggested, but he said he was now too exhausted to do the cleaning, let alone peel the celeriac, so we sat down at the kitchen table and drank the wine we'd bought for dinner while Alfie told us stories about his chequered past. Someone said, 'Alfie, put the kettle on.' And Alfie said, no, he didn't think it would suit him. I feel pretty limp myself now, and I wonder why that couple felt it necessary to stand talking bang in the middle of the narrowest point of Parkway between the flower stall and the electrical shop so no one could get by. As Alfie says, they could have asked each other to one another's houses and discussed all that over lunch. Why do I leave the shopping until Saturday when I could easily do it on Monday morning? Perhaps because it would be boring.

# Motorway madness

The magpies have been behaving strangely recently. Our local ones, who I thought were divorced, appeared together on the morning of the daughter's party, arranging themselves prettily in the tree outside the dining-room window and putting on a great show of mutual regard. Then we had to go all the way to Wales so that I could interview a man about his work. Every two or three miles a magpie would fly across the road – invariably from left to right. Not one chose to fly from right to left. On the way home exactly the same thing happened. I can only think they were the same magpies, had gone left to do whatever it is they do (carrion-eating mostly, I believe) and we caught them on their return journey. We passed one that had been run over and Janet said she wouldn't care to be the person who had squashed it. On the other hand it was fairly unlucky for the magpie.

Looking for somewhere to spend the night, our eye lit on a handsome black-and-white hotel standing alone in the middle of some roads. It was 6.30 pm and we hadn't had anything to eat since scrambled eggs in Moreton-in-the-Marsh early in the morning so we headed for the door with confident anticipation. It was locked and not a light was to be seen anywhere in the not-inconsiderable edifice. Thwarted, we prowled restlessly around, looking for signs of life as the evening drew on. Eventually Janet peered through the window of the proprietor's annexe. The proprietor was sitting in an easy chair, a glass clutched in her hand, her eyes glued to the television set, and *nothing* was going to shift her – certainly not two boring old would-be guests. The common attitude of English hoteliers is quite remarkable. I get the impression that most of them detest the human race and would prefer to be mortuary attendants and have a bit of peace. We drove on to the next town and looked at a few tariffs. Not being greatly taken by the prospect of steak, chips and peas or gammon, chips and peas or cod, peas and chips, we settled for a more up-market establishment of the Prawns Marie Rose, Duck a l'Orange and Black Forest Gâteau type. Not ideal but minimally preferable.

Seated at dinner, our attention was caught, inevitably, by the conversation at an adjacent table. Two ladies and a man were discussing their plans for the next day. From what we could gather he was going to spend the night in the car; he had brought his own cereal and said he needed only to add to it hot water from the tap in order to make it palatable. The elder lady revealed her intention of buying some lamb chops and making cauliflower cheese, and gave an account of her travels round the coast of Australia. The younger lady didn't say anything much. Janet and I, light-headed from hunger, couldn't hear between the lines. We couldn't for the life of us figure out the relationship between these people, or think why the man was sleeping in the car. It was extremely frustrating and served us right for eavesdropping. Lost in surmise, we grew hysterical with reprehensible mirth, dropped our napkins and swallowed our pudding the wrong way. We must have appeared completely mad, since we said scarcely anything to each other, merely giving occasional vent to hoots of maniacal laughter. This being the case, I got a considerable surprise when we had retired to the bar and a perfect stranger – an American gentleman – observed from the corner where he was sitting that we should write a weekly satirical column for a magazine. My mouth dropped open. Satirical may not be the *mot juste*, but it *is* weekly after all. Did he have second sight? Is rudeness in a restaurant sufficient justification for hanging out one's shingle as a satirist? Then he said his favourite book was Beryl's *Bottle Factory Outing* and it seemed like a small world.

Finally, crawling off to bed, we discovered that the bathroom had one of those relentless extractor fans. Janet turned off the light which is supposed eventually to

de-activate the thing, but it went on and on in a monotonously disapproving, positively Protestant fashion, reminding me irresistibly of the Reverend Ian Paisley. After about half an hour Janet said in a tone of muffled hysteria, 'What does it think's *happened* in there?' It did stop before morning, but by then the traffic had started up and we had to take to the road again and watch the magpies flying to the right. Our American friend had told us that he had been carried off an aeroplane some days before, hyper-ventilating, and I concluded that it's travelling that drives people mad. I'm going to stay in Camden Town for a while with my head in a paper bag. On the whole the magpies behave more rationally when they keep off the roads.

# April

# Huffing and puffing

The words *Das Betreten ist verboten* commonly have the opposite effect to that intended. 'Why not?' the citizen asks himself, plodding purposefully up and down on the grass. This perversity extends throughout the animal kingdom. The other morning I watched a bold blackbird eating the cats' meat from the cats' dish in the back yard, and Morgan, the cat of Janet's neighbour, climbed precariously up a dodgy sapling in order to eat the bit of bacon fat hung there for the birds.

I am thinking along these lines because I am absolutely sick of being hooked on cigarettes. I long to give up the habit, since I hate the idea of further enriching the tobacco barons, but I cannot bear the thought of incurring the approval of such as Edwina Currie. I know what would happen. Some health-food-consuming puritan would notice that I wasn't wreathed in the customary cloud of smoke and would congratulate me with a maddening smile. He would ask if I didn't feel much better now, and I would rush straight out to buy myself a Havana cigar a mile long. People of the most tiresome sort would assume I had joined their club. They would imagine I had taken their advice and I find the prospect insupportable. They never shut up in these circumstances, but lay claim to responsibility for your improved moral tone and wax brotherly like the worst sort of fundamentalist. Is it possible merely to give the appearance of being a defiant smoker? We went to a banquet the other evening and five people on our table puffed away throughout the meal, waiting with evil relish for the loyal toast and the words 'You may smoke'. It's like being given permission to breathe. I can't think why we've got such a bunch of bossy-boots running the country when the vast majority of us are averse to being told what to do and when to do it.

I watched open-mouthed a few days ago as Mrs Thatcher scooted round an open space whipping up bits of paper and stuffing them into a litter bag. We have mucky power-stations and conifer plantations despoiling the land and she doesn't say a squeak about them. She doesn't tell the petrol companies to cut out the lead or manufacturers to do something about the emissions that cause acid rain. Has she indeed said any word of disapprobation about the hamburger boxes and aerosols which are making walloping great holes in the ozone layer? No, I don't think so. Our leaders are all in too much of a tizz about our crisp packets and fag ends.

Admittedly a roomful of smoke is horrid for the non-smoker. One cigarette in a non-smoking household will permeate the atmosphere in a positively uncanny fashion from cellar to attic, and I am myself prejudiced against those who smoke in the bathroom. This being the case, I am in a splendid position to kick the habit since I am off to stay in just such a household. If I want to smoke I shall have to go and stand by the Atlantic. One of my hosts had a granny who used to smoke like a chimney and he would carry her over the snowdrifts, wrapped up in a duffelcoat, to the end of the garden, where she could consume gaspers to her heart's content. She lived to a ripe old age and was, I am told, a lovely colour, whether due to

'That's no' a snowman, that's Granny'

nicotine or all that fresh air is unclear. If you have to put on your hat and coat and wellies every time you want a fag it does have some deterrent effect, so I may come home purified. If only nobody goes out of his way to tell me what a good person I am. I'm taking my embroidery too. And while you can read and smoke and paint and smoke and write and smoke at the same time, I defy anybody to sew and smoke simultaneously. You need all the fingers you've got, and I never did get the hang of sticking a cigarette to the lower lip and squinting to keep the smoke out of the eyes. Perhaps now I'll never need to.

# Don't take it with you

It has often struck me as strange that we should have on the one hand mass unemployment and on the other a pressing shortage of domestic servants. Why do we not, I ask myself, hire ourselves out to each other as cooks-general, house-parlour maids, butlers and footmen? *And* gardeners and chauffeurs and governesses and laundry maids and little boys to clean the boots. It is more interesting tidying up other people's houses than one's own, and rather more rewarding cooking for other people's families – they are less likely to greet the *entrée* dish with dismissive cries of 'Oh no, not macaroni cheese *again*'. I have always thought that if (which heaven forfend) I should be left penniless and alone and had to earn a living, I should promptly apply for a position as housekeeper in some easily run – possibly bachelor – establishment set in rolling parkland. Before committing myself I should insist on ample free time in which to study the local wild life, and copious perks such as a fine old Oloroso in the evenings and the right to sell dripping at the back door. If I had the run of the library, and TV in my room (or suite if the house offered such an amenity), I shouldn't trouble at all about the lack of transport to the nearest town (a notorious barrier to the employment of skittish girls) and I should wear a *châtelaine* about my waist. If my employer proposed to marry somebody of whom I did not approve I should hand in my notice, and if he was the type of person – like one not a million miles from here – who would spray water over the sheet of paper I was writing on, I should put ground glass in his tapioca. Much more fun than working in a typing pool or packing frozen chickens.

However, these are day dreams. The actual, annual nightmare of spring cleaning is with us again and when I'm not wasting time building (easily run) castles in the air I'm wondering about the feasibility of buying a tent and living in it all by myself. Possessions are hell. They need variously to be washed, dusted, polished, mended with glue or darned with wool, or kept in the safe. With the major ones you have to pay enormous sums in rates and replace the tiles on the roof. Possessions leak, buckle, rot, get lost or stolen, come to pieces in your hands or fall down about your ears. They leave little time for you to do more amusing things, and cause you to grow old before your time.

I know some people who are keen on boats – which are, I suppose, a sort of water-borne tent – and for a moment I wondered again about the possibilities of living in one of them, but as Zélide has pointed out, at one time people had to be knocked on the head in dark alleys and press-ganged in order to be persuaded to go to sea, and conditions haven't changed all that much. What might be a dinky little cabin on a fine day can turn into the Little Ease with no trouble at all as you find yourself miles out of port, sleeping in wet oilskins while scurvy sets in because you forgot to stow the cox's orange pippins in the dunnage. And if, for some reason, you refuse to set out to sea from the marina, you end up sitting on the pontoon amidst the duck muck staring gloomily at the far horizon reflecting on past mutinies and the consequences thereof. My grandpapa was a sea captain and so is my step-brother, but he seems to have disappeared. Then you start thinking about making an enormous fortune and perhaps buying a *bigger* boat, and you're back into possessions and the infinite trouble they involve. There is some tiresome, immutable law about the space you live in and the way you fill it up. Palace or hovel, sooner or later it will start to overflow with bargains you couldn't resist, old newspapers you can't throw away, and the thing with knobs on that your auntie left you.

After a while, thinking along these lines, you inevitably begin to muse wistfully on the tomb – one shroud (no need for a change in the locker), your wedding ring and a lock of hair from the head of your best beloved, and you're away. Yet here again you must exercise thought if you wish to be left undisturbed, and implore your relations not to fling any unconsidered trifles in with you out of misplaced sentiment. Rossetti did that. Overcome with grief and the certainty that All Was Over he buried a book of his unpublished poems with *his* best beloved, and after a year or two, as inspiration seemed to be lacking, he dug her up and fished them out again. I do that sort of thing all the time. Janet made me throw some old clothes away and I spent hours hunting through the Oxfam shop looking for them. If anybody finds a man's Dior shirt with a poloneck I want it back.

Perhaps the simplest move would be to set out to sea without fussing about the dodgy sea-cock and just quietly go down – with all hands.

# At the crossroads

As I go down for the third time under a tidal wave of books, clothes, papers, letters, bills, teenagers, cats and all manner of things I've never used and don't know the purpose of (where did that lidless double saucepan come from? I've never seen it before and if anybody thinks I'm going to start mincing around making hollandaise and delicate little uncurdled custards they can – to put it at its mildest – start thinking again), I reflect yet further on order and simplicity. Why is everything such a *mess*? Leicester for a start. It's been buggered about like almost every other British town I can remember and I wonder why. And the motorways. What a shambles. And our system of signposting. I like signposts when they appear at the appropriate junction and tell the truth, but this happens too seldom. In Scotland, for example, the erectors of signposts seem reluctant to reveal to the motorist the precise whereabouts of Dumfries. It is not that one is eager to visit this town – which is doubtless no less buggered about than anywhere else – but one needs to know where it is in order to circumvent it. Then, on the other hand, Hinckley and Nebo are the two best-signposted places I've ever come across. I've never been to Hinckley and I don't want to go there, but as you travel north its existence is advertised every few miles. We did visit Nebo once, out of curiosity, and as far as I remember the main street comprised a cottage, a chapel and a chicken coop: not a place, one would have thought, sufficiently significant to justify the plethora of signposts, although I believe the original Nebo was one of the Cities of the Plain. I wonder what its signposting situation was like. Surely no honest Israelite would have wished to call there.

We rattled to Leicester the other day, driving along the M1 negotiating our way through the cones and listening with careful apprehension to the noises the old banger was making. I've never yet had to spend the night on the hard shoulder and I kept telling myself it would be a new, if disorderly, experience. However, we arrived in one piece, whereupon I found I'd forgotten my cheque book, so our guest, whom we'd invited along for a treat, had to foot the bill for tea and supper. The occasion was a performance of Strindberg's *Easter*, starring our Jemma. As we took our seats I reflected that if I was in Jemma's shoes they would now be scrambling on to the next bus out of town, but I needn't have worried. She was magnificent. And what was even better from my point of view – for I am one who suffers agonies of vicarious suffering and it is this that usually keeps me away from the theatre – she didn't forget her lines or fall over the furniture. If I was an actor I should secrete a cyanide pill in my doublet for fear of these eventualities, but the entire cast sailed triumphantly to a splendid conclusion and I clapped till I was hoarse – as it were.

What was surprising was that the play had a happy ending, which is not a thing I usually associate with Strindberg. I expect him to conclude in a disorderly fashion with everyone being dragged off in strait jackets, clutching their throats and shrieking indignantly about quite minor matters. I was relieved when Eleonore was not sent back to the asylum and the family was permitted to retain its household effects.

As we rattled back along the M1 I thought about signposts again – the ones along Life's Highway – and how one keeps missing them. If I'd had the brains of a rat, I thought to myself, I would have stayed in the convent where one has no possessions apart from one's bed and one's teeth. If I had been, not a nun, but an actress, I would have been able to rely on cues to guide me. I would have had a structure, a set and a director. I would have had a dressing-room (very like a cell in its minimal and temporary quality) a green room (very like the nuns' recreation room – or indeed the prisoners' association room) and be instructed where to be and at what time to be at it. I would not have been my own person with all the attendant responsibilities. Also, I would have been constrained to behave – or perform – well; and there isn't all that much difference between the two.

True freedom, I have decided gloomily, is a concomitant of virtue, of humility and obedience – not to our political leaders – but to certain rules of which we are all cognisant but which we choose to ignore. If I could only define precisely what they are I could advise the rest of you where to turn off and where to persevere, and I would have felt like a useful signpost. As it is, I can only grovel at the crossroads, peering at the map and roaring at my fellow travellers who insist on carrying round as much useless luggage as I do myself and then storing it in their attics.

# Buffet garni

I saw a man recently on TV suggesting that chimpanzees should be reclassified as hominids. When I mentioned this in passing to my friend the analyst he said that if they did that they might also consider the possibility of relegating certain people to the ranks of the Great Apes. I've already made a little list – headed by those who run British Rail. Many of us have long been dissatisfied with BR for diverse reasons. It seems to be run by men of a Machiavellian cunning and complexity of mind or, in the new dispensation, by a bunch of monkeys. Why, for instance, does one have to trudge along the platform dragging one's luggage (the porter race seems to be extinct) and clutching one's second-class ticket, past dozens of empty first-class carriages (empty, that is, except for a few men with Samsonite briefcases, and some Japanese and Germans) in order to cram oneself into a second-class compartment with far too many of one's fellow hominids for comfort? Apes in overcrowded circumstances lose condition, go off their food, bang their heads aimlessly against the wall, and their fur falls out. Is it not expensive in fuel and energy to haul these empty first-class carriages the length and breadth of the country? Why is it cheaper to buy a return, rather than a single, ticket? Why are there so many different sorts of tickets – away-day ones and fare-saver ones and ones that you collect off the backs of soap packets? Why are we not told more clearly which of these methods is the most economical? And why can't you drink the water? Some friends in the country, having to be in London for a wedding, booked first-class tickets on an early train and were assured that there would be a buffet-car to hand. Of course there wasn't; and when they asked the ticket collector for a glass of water to wash down some medically essential pills he strongly advised them against it. And why does the guard keep pressuring us over the loudspeaker not to leave our personal belongings on board? Most of us won't, and those of us who are chronically absent-minded will, since that is the nature of absent-mindedness. Our mothers, wives and friends have not succeeded in curing us of the habit despite constant reminders, so why does the guard imagine he will succeed where others have failed? And why is the train late?

The other day the third son and I had to travel to Wales for an overnight stay. We walked the customary half mile down the platform to our second-class carriage and found seats. I sat next to somebody who hadn't washed for some considerable time, so when the son suggested that we should avail ourselves of the buffet-car facilities I agreed (I don't usually). There was no room in the second-class section, so we asked if we could trespass on the first-class one and were told we could. We couldn't see much difference between the two except for anti-macassars or something, but when the ticket-collector came along he said we had to pay extra. This was sufficiently annoying, but what really irritated me beyond endurance was the menu. Let me demonstrate: 'Smoked Salmon with Lemon and Brown Bread and Butter, £2.95. A touch of luxury to start your meal while enjoying your journey.' I wasn't enjoying the beastly journey. I wasn't, I wasn't. They go on to describe absolutely everything with more adjectives than a Bodice Ripper writer. Adjectives and porn seem inseparable as Siamese twins. 'Chilled Fruit Juice, 70p. Please choose from our selection of orange, grapefruit, tomato or farm-pressed English apple juice.' Do they fear we might imagine the train had squashed the apples? 'Oxtail Soup, £1.25. A bowl of rich, hot Old English Oxtail Soup garnished with diced beef.' Oh shut up, Jules, and just open the tin. Anyway, *how* 'Old'? 'Shredded Carrots Vinaigrettes. In a specially created French dressing.' How specially created? Did they stand on their heads in the engine while tossing it together? 'Waldorf. Our own recipe of chopped celery, red apple, walnuts and creamed mayonnaise sauce.' What do they mean – 'our' recipe? That's *the* recipe for this tiresome salad. And the Marquise potatoes are actually 'baked in the oven until golden brown'. Very original that. What a good idea. The *oven*, already. Why not the fridge? Everything is described variously as plump, rich, light, crisp, young, fluffy, tender, fresh or juicy. A hint of sadism (like the hint of nutmeg in the Dauphinoise potatoes) creeps in with 'boned', 'grated', 'chopped' and 'sliced', and it all gave me acute indigestion. Even the tea is described as 'Freshly Brewed'. Fancy that. As for the wine list – well, I just offer one example: 'Liebfraumilch Prinz Rupprecht. Clean and very fruity with a mellow easy-to-drink style.' Is this to reassure us that it need not be syphoned down the throat while the guard holds your nose? It might take the apes some time to write the whole of Shakespeare but it looks to me as though they could make a start with the BR menu.

# May

# Murder most tasteful

There is a certain expression which actors assume when the director has decided that the only possible way he can force his film to make sense is to use the *flashback*. The moment I saw the young soldier adopting a faintly shifty, glazed look I knew he was going to fall down in a fit, and that then we should have the bang and the crump and the splosh of trench warfare. Don't ask me why it wouldn't be sufficient for him merely to remark, 'God, it was hell in the trenches. Every time I think of it it makes me go all queer.' I don't think film directors are very fond of words; it's the cameraman they wish to keep happy, and to do this they must let him demonstrate his skills.

The film was *Ryan's Daughter* and it did not hold my attention. This may be why I didn't understand it; also I was simultaneously reading Agatha Christie – an economical device which means I can watch the same films and read the same books quite frequently since I don't remember what happened, and I get the plots confused. Hercule Poirot running about the coasts of Ireland in his little shiny shoes, and John Mills gibbering round the body in the library. I kept thinking the film had ended, but then the cameraman saw another shot he simply must have and it went on. At one point I hoped the rather tiresome heroine was going to be tarred and feathered but she only had her hair cut. And was that man with the Irish accent Kirk Douglas or Burt Lancaster or somebody quite else? I was told by a more alert family member who the villains were (this was established by their shooting somebody in the back) but they seemed harmless enough after that and I couldn't quite see why the heroine was unfaithful to Kirk Lancaster when she'd gone to the lengths of proposing to him.

I am thinking about film-making since it has been suggested that I write one and I don't know how to go about it. Action is called for, and plentiful surprises. It isn't enough to have a number of characters sitting round discussing the meaning of the Universe. Horses are called for, pitched battles and passionate scenes in ballrooms; movement and colour and not too much chat; flashbacks; and grist to the mill of the cameraman. One needs to change one's way of looking at things. I suppose if I were really smart I could suggest setting a film in somewhere warm and exotic – India, the Bahamas – but things would still have to happen, and I don't suppose my presence would be essential, so there wouldn't be any point. I might as well set it here. I've already got into a frightful muddle working out a plot. There are said to be seven basic ones and I think I've got them all in – plus several ghosts and a mad axeman. The wish not to bore the pants off the public can be taken too far, as in 'Cecil B. de Mille / rather against his will / was persuaded to leave Moses / out of the Wars of the Roses'. I always thought that rather funny, but now it doesn't seem so amusing. I don't want everybody to be reading *Murder at the Vicarage* while my epic runs its course. We want them glued to the screen, laughing, crying and shuddering with terror, don't we? And then we come to another problem. I prefer the nasty bits to happen off-stage (*ne coram populo*, etc.) and learn from a messenger that somebody has just put his own eyes out, or somebody else has sliced up his sister. I don't want actually to witness these events. Nor do I care to witness people in transports in the bedroom, and the last film I saw was crammed with undressed ladies and gentlemen variously caressing or carving each other up. My approach is not fashionable. I liked those films where every time anybody opened a cupboard a body fell out. Murder had occurred, but we hadn't been constrained to watch it in the process.

If we don't have any flashbacks or spurts of blood or naked flesh will anybody watch? I think it might be safer to write a play about a snooker player, and then everybody can just watch the game – which is what they'd probably be doing anyway.

# Looking on the bright side

I have received a timely letter from an enchanting and brave lady in Amsterdam chiding me gently for being dismissive about possessions. It was especially timely because not only was I fed up with all the *things* collecting dust, rusting, and harbouring moths; I was getting very impatient with the *person*. Hauling the corpse out of bed in the morning I found myself reflecting that I'd brushed its hair and its teeth and buckled up its shoes more times than I care to remember. I'd washed it, dressed it, and put its eyeliner on day after day for years and years, and not only that, I was supposed to be responsible for its liver and kidneys and its lungs and heart. It was the temple of my soul and I shouldn't really be flooding it with Pils and kippering it with Silk Cut. It had stood by me through thick and thin and deserved a little consideration, not the irritation with which I was presently regarding it. If God hadn't seen fit to make me pure spirit, it wasn't for me to complain.

My correspondent in Holland put a new perspective on all this dissatisfaction. She was imprisoned by the Nazis during the war for being in the first organised resistance group, and in jail she had to wear '...their beastly (and most uncomfortable) prison clothes; prickly underwear as well as dress and apron. Prickly owing to wood splinters in the fibre.' Then when she was freed in May 1945 she had one suitcase containing her few remaining possessions '...precious food given us by kind French soldiers, my own clothes and, all the letters I had received while in jail (one every six weeks), my bible and a few books'. She sat on this suitcase all the way home until prevailed upon 'in spite of vehement protests' to leave it in the army bus which was to take her and her companions to The Hague, while she had a proper meal with a Dutch army unit in their barracks, and when she finally got home she discovered that a hole had been cut in her suitcase and she no longer had any possessions at all.

Very early this morning Someone noticed a tramp sleeping in the garden with his head in the pink weeds which are proliferating everywhere this year. He had nothing of his own and had put down a bin-liner on the flag stones to protect his body a little from the night chill. That also made me feel remarkably small in between wondering what on earth sort of society we have evolved. I don't remember many people sleeping in the garden in the bad old days. Our mattress may need replacing – its skeleton is sticking through its skin in places – but with a little manoeuvring we spend warm, comfortable nights. I waste an inordinate amount of time fussing about my 1890 satin patchwork quilt which needs skilful mending, but all I need to do is persuade Someone to hand over a number of his old ties, and then prevail upon Janet to cut them up and sew them on, and the thing will be as good as new. I really must put aside all these trivial anxieties and pull myself together.

As my correspondent also reminds me, this is a pleasant time of year: 'And talking about beauty – just now – last week, this week and perhaps next week – the trees on our canals are indescribably lovely: some like the one just in front of my windows, extravagantly full in blossom, with a tender green unfolding on the elms. Whether against a grey sky or huge sailing clouds and a bright blue sky, this green is sheer joy from early morning until late dusk.' She is two months older than the century. I've got a rioting clematis to look at, and an azalea and the aforesaid pink weeds with the tramp in them, and forget-me-nots and wild geranium, but all I notice is the rhododendron which is far from well and the broken snails. Every morning a depressing mixture of shell and the squashy bits lies all over the flag stones, and I stare at them gloomily, wondering how they got that way. I know it can't be people walking on them because people don't. They like squashing puff balls and popping seaweed but no one in his right mind puts his foot on a snail. It is not a pleasant sensation. I conclude it must be the birds. I'm not seeing the charm in them at the moment either. One of the little bastards tapped at my window the other morning and I do so wish they wouldn't do that, and the rest of them relieve themselves on the lilac leaves. I suppose if beauty is in the eye of the beholder so are dead snails and bird crap, and the probable reason I'm developing an increasing resemblance to W.C. Fields is that I've been mean to my liver. I think I'll toss the beer cans into the neighbour's garden and sit down and think on those things that are lovely and of good report.


# There be dragons


We have conducted several luncheon parties recently sitting on the step between the gate posts gazing up and down the street. This is because some of our guests have had the temerity to drive here in their motor cars and the towing-away lorries are based just at the top of our crescent.

These lorries remind me of nothing so much as the dragons of yore. Dragons used to sit in their lairs until they fancied a maiden or two, whereupon they would make a sudden sally, seize upon their prey and return, licking their chops, to their fetid dens leaving the populace in an uproar, wringing its hands and wailing. This is exactly what happens now when the marauder bears down on an innocent vehicle. Tremendous scenes of passion and violence occur, but the lorries are deaf and insensible to pleas and threats alike, and if I was them I should exercise great caution for fear of bringing upon myself a person on a white horse with a plume in his hat. Even when we dare to eat in the usual way round the dining-room table we have to station a look-out on the balcony, and meals are

67

constantly disrupted as drivers leap out to defend their property.

What is so exasperating about it is that the threatened cars are doing no harm at all; causing no obstructions, blocking no exits. The crescent is sufficiently wide for traffic to flow smoothly, and anyway there isn't all that much of it. No, the point is, dragons are notoriously lazy and loath to wander too far in furtherance of their satisfactions. They clear their immediate vicinity of maidens before venturing further afield. Besides where the maidens are really thick on the ground there's no room for them to manoeuvre. The towing-away lorries can't get to the congested spots because, even if they managed to get in and make their haul, they'd never get away again, so they wreak havoc among the (comparatively) peaceful meadows and glades of Camden Town and the citizenry is disconsolate. Mismanagement I call it.

And then there's British Telecom. One of our telephones doesn't work at all and another has been dropped and makes a funny noise when it rings, so we requested some new ones – ages ago. After a while we rang BT – a protracted and enervating business involving speaking to one department who tell you to speak to another department who refer you back to the number you first thought of, i.e. the previous department – and after some discussion we learned that they hadn't got any telephones, not the sort we wanted anyway. We should ring again in a few weeks and ask if they'd got them in. As Janet remarked in a rather high-pitched tone (I'd made her conduct this interview), you don't expect to have to ring up the fishmonger to ask if he's got any fish. Then *she* made a funny noise.

And then there's London Transport. I had to travel on the Broad Street line a few days ago – I couldn't go by car

because the streets were blocked by towing-away lorries –
and after I'd waited for half an hour the tannoy
announced negligently that the 17.20 to Richmond had
been cancelled. Just like that. Just the bald announcement
and then profound silence. Eventually a train did bowl in
and far too many of us struggled on to it. After a while a
disembodied voice remarked over the intercom that its
wheels were coming off and it was going to stop at
Willesden, where we must all disembark, so that this defect
could be remedied. Nobody rioted and I am impressed at
the self-control of the much-abused British public.

69

And then there's the Church. I went to Confession last Saturday. Or rather I tried. I made the usual excuses to myself about how I didn't need to go yet. Not really. I could wait until I felt the mists of death darkening my sight and then rush round in the nick of time. I fought against these temptings of the Evil One and walked into Church and sat down. I waited. Several other sinners were waiting too. Time passed; the box stood empty. After a while a wee nun went round to the presbytery to ask where the priests were. The priests, she was told, had gone to the Cathedral to see one of their number ordained. She came back and told us and we all went home again, unshriven. I expect the priests had been towed away from the Cathedral precincts. I expect they couldn't get through on the telephone to inform the congregation. I expect they couldn't get on the train because its wheels had come off. I expect purgatory, or possibly hell, will very much resemble life in late twentieth-century England.

# A ripping good day

We were caught in a traffic jam last weekend. I had forgotten how boring this could be and was extremely glad that our friend Chip was among those present. The third son, who was driving, tried to alleviate the tedium by playing music, which roared out from behind me with the overall effect of a pile-driver. Voices were raised and things were said in the heat of the moment. I learned that

'Latest thing, Madame — our Eezi-Rip Bodice'

I was the most appalling passenger the world had ever known, and the son learned a few things about ungrateful children and vipers' teeth. When we got bored with arguing with each other, the son suggested that Jemma should roll down her window and tell the man alongside, in the car towing the caravan, that we were hard pushed to know which were uglier – his children, his wife or his dog. I advised against this, as there was no chance of making a quick get-away.

At last we reached the country lanes and passed through a village called Deverills, agreeing that this would be the correct sort of name for some characters in a bodice-ripper – Wolf Deverill, the ageing rake with a son, Jasper, who bids fair to be as dissolute as his father; Gloriana Deverill, the eldest daughter with flashing eyes and a seat like a man's as she flings her stallion at the walls and fences in pursuit of the fox; Petal Deverill, the youngest daughter, winsome, with brimming violet eyes and a deep sense of shame as she contemplates the rest of her family.

The delightful thing about all this was that Chip, who moves in a more elevated sphere of literature, had not previously been familiar with the term bodice-ripper, although he was aware of the genre. We had a long debate about the ethics of bodice-ripping – who was allowed to rip and who got ripped. The rules are subtle but binding. Could a person, for instance, rip his wife's bodice, asked Chip. Only, we responded, if she was estranged from him and had locked herself in the West Wing. Highwaymen and the male Deverills could rip bodices, but Sir Caspar Milquetoast certainly couldn't. Gloriana would get her bodice ripped but retaliate with a horse-whip before succumbing to the next stage. Petal would get her bodice a little bit ripped but be rescued in the nick of time. Housemaids and dairy maids, on the whole, didn't get their bodices ripped because they were jolly, voluptuous, accommodating wenches who didn't need much persuasion and unlaced their own bodices with sly, inviting glances. The next question was – what precisely constituted a bodice? It is the top half of a frock, usually closely fitting, and there aren't many around at the moment. (I do not mean that women are going around half-clad like Page Three Girls, but that frocks now tend to be looser and made in one piece.) It is not the same thing as the Chilprufe Liberty Bodice, a strange ribbed (rather than ripped) garment with dangling suspenders which mothers once made their daughters wear.

Having established this, we arrived at our destination. It had been unpleasantly hot in the car while we were stuck in the traffic jam, the sky a bright blue with – as the son remarked – some very poorly executed clouds in it looking like a bad painting. When we got out, all that had changed. The sky was now gun-metal grey and a wind had risen. Seduced by the early promise of the day, our hosts had arranged lunch under the dovecote and we all had to be issued with extra woollies. Lunch itself consisted of pigeon pie, which was very delicious, but there weren't any doves in the dovecote and it seemed a little poignant. We sat on the grass reflecting on our food taboos and why we never eat things we really hate – snakes, rats, lizards, scorpions, etc. – but creatures you could get quite fond of if you knew them well. The children of the house, it seemed, had declined the pie because they *had* known the pigeons quite well. It all went along with the irrationality of the rules of bodice-ripping. As did the way we stayed stubbornly shivering under the dovecote, because this was the country in England in summer and that's what it's for. There was a perfectly good Palladian pile we could have been sitting in, but we stuck it out till the last minute, when it began to rain. Then we agreed that it was this very irrationality which has made our island race what it is, and we all drove home again.

# June

# Vital statistics

The daughter came in the other day and said she'd just brushed shoulders with a person bent on killing himself. She had been in one of those curious shops which suit all requirements, and somebody she described as a hippy had bought two cans of Coke and a bottle of Paracetamol.

I worried about it for a second or two until the kettle boiled, and then I noticed that the daughter was trying to persuade her brother to let her try out on him a new wrestling hold she had just learned. Being the only girl in the family, she has evolved what can be described as a *positive* approach to life. She would not have gone down well in a Victorian drawing-room. After a while she observed loftily that women live longer than men, and her brother said not if they were killed when they were young they didn't.

I had been considering this very question of longevity and wondering about possible antidotes. I have read that overdosing on Paracetamol is a bad idea: it doesn't kill you quite, and you start bleeding from the ears – among other undesirable side-effects. Shooting yourself in the head is usually, though not invariably, a successful means of getting off the stage, but women tend not to shoot themselves in the head because it ruins the make-up. They attempt to shoot themselves in the heart; and whereas most people have no trouble locating their head, the heart is a different matter. Most of us imagine it is situated well to the left while, in fact it is, I believe, more in the middle, so unless you use an elephant gun and blow yourself to bits you could end up merely perforated.

Thinking about this, I began to worry about Bess, the landlord's daughter, the landlord's black-eyed daughter. As far as I remember, she was waiting for her friend the Highwayman to come riding, riding, riding when the road was a ribbon of moonlight over the something moor, but the then equivalent of the Old Bill were lying in wait for him, and for some unguessable reason they lashed poor Bess to a musket. I suppose it was a sadistic jest on the part of the brutal and licentious soldiery, but I don't see the point. They tied her to her narrow bed, and tied the musket beneath her breast, which already sounds to me too far to the left – or even, if they got it quite wrong, too far to the right – and then they sat down and looked out of the casement and waited. Meanwhile, by dint of wriggling a bit, Bess got her finger on the trigger, and when she heard the pounding of coconut shells she pulled it.

Now there are several loose ends here. If you can imagine tying somebody to a musket, it seems to me you would position it in the middle of them, especially if you were a trooper, since military men are known to have a preference for the symmetrical. Then a lot depends on the height of Bess. Was the butt of the musket resting on the floor? How high is a musket? Supposing it to be centrally situated, was it angled to get her in the vitals, and if so how? I don't think the poet had thought it through here. It seems to me that if the barrel of the musket was tied so that it rested between her cleavage, then when she pulled the trigger she would merely blow off the tip of her nose. But the most puzzling thing of all is still the troopers' precise

77

reason for doing such a deed. If they wanted to make sure that Bess wouldn't warn her friend, all they had to do was lock her in the cupboard – or shoot her themselves while the coast was clear. If her passion for this Highwayman was so widely known that the troopers believed she would die to warn him of their presence, why didn't they make sure she couldn't get at the trigger? Anyway, why were these brute-like troopers so romantically inclined as to suppose that she would? I wouldn't. When they embarked on this action they must have entertained the possibility, and if the arrest of the Highwayman was such a priority with the authorities that they assigned a platoon of troopers to sit up all night in order to apprehend him, didn't they realise that it was no time for practical jokes? Their superiors must have been furious when they discovered what had happened.

Still, many poets are mad or drunk or on something, and some just don't think. A lot of them kill themselves, or die young from other causes, and if they live to be very old their melancholy increases. I wonder if the daughter's hippy had a slim volume tucked away somewhere in a drawer. How terribly, terribly sad everything is. I think I'll write a poem.

# A sparrow falls

The other day the fifth son was hit on the head by a bird. He was sitting on the top of a bus – not on the outside, you understand – on the top floor fo'rard. I haven't been on a bus for years but he tells me they have a new sort now with windows that open in front. So there he was thinking about the exam he was about to take, when this bird was swept in through the open window and struck him on the head causing some shock to the nervous system. Its impetus carried it past him on to the seat behind, which chanced to be unoccupied, and when he had recovered sufficiently he turned to see how it was. It too had sustained a bad shock and was lying on its back with its eyes half closed and its feet pointing skywards. It was, he tells me, a smallish manky looking bird and its feathers were all wet, but he didn't feel he could just leave it there so he picked it up in a newspaper and bore it with him to the lower deck. Here he was accosted by a fellow passenger who asked what living thing it was that he was carrying, and when the son explained the man cried out with pity and took it from him. The last the son saw was the man cradling this horrid, sodden bird with its little scaly feet, and addressing the tenderest endearments to it. I think that a pretty tale.

The oddest thing about it, according to the son, was the species of bird, which may have been a starling or, on the other hand, may have been a sparrow. He says it is usually pigeons which are hit by buses. I always used to think it was foolish of pigeons to walk across roads when they could fly, but I had failed to take into account the fact that they could find themselves on the same flight path as the top of a bus.

Some statistics were published recently about the mortality rate of small creatures in this country. Thousands and thousands of them bite the dust each year. Those that are not hit by buses are taken out by the domestic cat. As I imagine many of these small creatures are rats and mice, I couldn't quite understand the censorious note in the text accompanying the statistics.

Catching rats and mice is what cats are for. It is sad when they catch songbirds, but they have little moral sense and cannot distinguish between what man does and does not want them to kill. Puss and Cadders no longer attempt to kill anything except, occasionally, each other, because I tend to leave them in London when we go to the country and while the city birds fall foul of the buses they seem to have the measure of the cats. Puss and Cadders though are dreadful in the country where, I have to admit, they wreak quite unnecessary havoc among little beasts and birds and carry them variously fluttering, squeaking and wriggling into the house. Many the baby rabbit, mole, vole, shrew and field mouse that we have tried to nurse back to health and many the time we have failed. Nor have we had any conspicuous success with wounded birds. I remember one in particular who flew into the lintel of the cottage door, just managed to make it back to a tree, and hung upside down, clutching a twig with one claw while we stood beneath holding out a tea towel in case it fell. We worried ourselves sick about that bird and I finally had to convince the children that God had his eye on the sparrow; it said so in Holy Scripture, and we could go in and have tea, leaving it to Him – a course I increasingly take since I have a craven inability to put things out of their misery. I cannot wring necks and we don't keep chloroform in the house. Just as well since one might be tempted to put oneself out of one's own misery. The rhododendron is looking desperately ill and in sore need of the *coup de grâce*, but I can't even bring myself to uproot it, suffering as I am at present from a form of oriental fatalism which I must have picked up somewhere when my resistance was lowered.

Telling oneself that all is the Will of God is a heresy that can lead to all manner of temporal inconveniences such as paying the same bill twice, submitting to unjust tax demands, and not looking for the little green man before you cross the road thus meeting the same fate as the pigeons. I do hope that the son's fellow passenger had more luck with the bird than we have ever had, and if its case seems hopeless I hope he has the requisite moral fibre to wring its neck. And, in passing, where does one procure chloroform?

# Table talk

Someone has long felt the need of a table of his own to sit and work at and leave his manuscripts on. In the past he has used the dining-room table, on occasions the kitchen table, and two trestle tables pushed together in his study. None of these arrangements has proved entirely satisfactory, especially as I use the far end of the kitchen table myself to keep unanswered post, unconsulted diaries and unpaid bills on. Not to mention the fruit bowl and the cat. So when, the other morning, he said the time had come to stop discussing the possibilities of buying him a table of his own and to go out and do it, none of us demurred.

He and I and Beryl and Janet climbed into the car and took off, leaving Gladys Mary and Graham neck-deep in Welsh lore at the dining-room table. We visited a North London warehouse where wardrobes, dressing-tables and cocktail cabinets occupied all the available floor space and the only table was a repro Regency number. This was discouraging and I was inclined to go home again, particularly as it was eleven o'clock and I was expecting a luncheon guest at 12.30, but Beryl and Someone were by now stirred by that thrill of the chase familiar to all who prefer second-hand furniture. I am not immune to it myself and have never bought a new piece of furniture in my life – it would be like shooting a sitting duck or a tethered goat, and no fun at all – but I have learned to pass by on the other side when I glimpse, out of the corner of my eye, steamer chairs which need only a little re-caning (five quid the chair, ninety-five the re-caning), occasional tables with a leg missing and spavined prams. Telling myself that I was long cured of impulse-buying (as I believe it is known), I followed the others into the car.

Unfortunately, we had chosen the one hot day for this expedition (I think it was June 11th) and creeping through the roadworks of London amongst all the rest of the traffic was unenjoyable. When we finally reached the other side of the river I had already started to winge and my other reaction to shopping trips – sales-resistance – had established itself. I was outnumbered and outclassed, so, unless I wanted to sit in the street in the sun like a foreigner, I had to trail round the depository (three floors) with the enthusiasts. It was only a month or two since I'd been there before, buying a desk for the fifth son, and a rug for his father. Then I had been tempted to forget about this useful desk and buy for the same price a life-size Samurai warrior constructed of a greenish metal. He was still there and I still liked him just as much, but you can't go mad and buy things in the presence of three other people. It is a solitary insanity. Beryl clearly felt the same constraint for she kept a close grip on herself. I had always known that the minute she clapped eyes on the nineteenth-century dentist's chair she would fall hopelessly in love with it and she did. I hadn't

been sure about the hat stand composed of a carved bear holding a tree with another smaller bear in its upper branches, but she stood by it silently for some time and I'm almost certain she was wondering how it would agree with Eric, the stuffed water buffalo who occupies her hallway. I was no better. I had to drag myself away from a brightly painted umbrella-stand representing the infant Hercules strangling a serpent – the serpent served as a retaining bar to hold the umbrellas upright – which would have stood by the front door and prevented it opening fully. There were fair-ground horses, a red telephone box, bits of spiral staircases, a wooden saint, marvellously awful Victorian pictures, dressers, a set of drawers from a chemist's shop with Latin names on the labels, two life-size wooden deer, an old illustrated lavatory pan – even the odd cocktail cabinet – but hardly any tables: the usual repro Regency number, of course, and a large oak table which was big enough for our purpose but apart from that had little else to recommend it. We said we'd think about it and left.

A hundred yards down the road we passed another warehouse with a large sign saying Trade Only prominently displayed over the door. Just inside the door, hanging on the wall were the legs and side bits of an enormous table – they looked perfect. The owner forgot all his strictures about Trade Only, dug out the top and sold it to Someone for a laughable sum. Next week when I feel stronger, I might tell you how we got this table into the study. But I'll never tell you where the warehouses are because one of you might go and buy my Samurai before I've saved up enough to buy him myself. And I might have to buy one for my luncheon guest who waited for long enough and then went home.

# Whose toothbrush?

We've been trying to bring some order into our lives. I've answered several letters – though by no means all I should have done – and Someone has his new table. It measures ten foot by four and a bit and had to be hauled up the front of the house by means of block-and-tackle and manoeuvred in through the window. The minute we saw it I knew it wouldn't go up the stairs, but the men who brought it found out the hard way. They suggested sawing it in half and then sticking it together again *in situ*, but happily our builder, John, scorned this craven ploy and chose the heroic way. I couldn't bear to watch. Removing whole windows and lugging hundredweights of mahogany around on ropes is man's work – quite exciting but implicit with disaster. The table now looks as though it had been there for a century or so and is already filling up with papers. Here's the rub. *All* flat surfaces fill up with something: usually with papers but also with cardigans, umbrellas, ghetto blasters, crisp packets, nail-varnish-remover, handbags and jugs of wilting bouquets.

When I speak of John as 'our builder' I do not mean somebody who once did some building for us. The house stands in need of constant adjustment, and John and we will be together, on a more or less occasional basis, until death do us part. Not long ago I decided we needed some flat surfaces in the bathrooms to put things on. I don't know why I did so decide, because I know better. I knew these little shelves would instantly be filled with things, and they were. I had a dim housewifely conviction that we should keep spare soap, loo rolls, bath cleaner and toothpaste in the places they would be needed, while what we now have, in fact, is: top shelf – a jar containing two dead conventional toothbrushes, one funny-looking one and two dead throw-away razors, a packet of dental floss, a bottle of nail-varnish remover and somebody's vanity bag; second shelf – a dried-up sponge, a container of eye-shadow, a jar of Bergamot and Royal Jelly, a battery shaver (defunct), a bowl of shaving soap, a carton of hair-colourer, a plastic jar with polka dots on (empty), two shaving brushes, a bottle of some decongestant, antihistamine analgesic, another dried-up sponge and two cartons of talcum powder; bottom shelf – two half-used tubes of toothpaste, a bar of soap (good), a china jar containing nine toothbrushes, an eye-lash brush and a thing for rubbing dead skin off people's feet, a pot of deodorant, some Wild Orchid body lotion, a jar of mouth-wash, a jar of elderflower water, a jar of henna, a jar of Hungary water, *my* toothbrush, a dead throw-away razor, two sachets of Evening Primrose skin-toner, a box of eye make-up, a bottle of baby lotion and a dead paint brush, and I've just noticed some nail varnish and some more nail-varnish remover concealed behind the baby lotion. Apart from my toothbrush, I have no idea who all these things pertain to since, by the very nature of bathrooms, I never get to see anybody using them. It is fairly obvious that most of them never are used as they are drying out or congealing according to their substance, but I don't like to just throw them away. I sometimes think I should muster the entire household and display each item separately to be claimed or summarily discarded. The trouble is our bathrooms are very small. To get the whole family in they'd have to stand on each other's shoulders in the bath. And while we are frequently all together for Sunday lunch it would seem inappropriate to use the occasion to reunite all those orphaned toothbrushes with their erstwhile owners. I should have to bring them downstairs and they would look very strange and squalid adjacent to the roast chicken. I really see no solution to the problem.

The fifth son must have a new toothbrush because he has just had his teeth cleaned and polished and must keep up the good work. This operation cost £6 and, as the son is still studying, the government is prepared to pay the sum: only, in order to get our hands on the money, we have to fill in an enormous form 'for people with not much money coming in'. This phrase might just as well read 'for people with not much between the ears', as it is full of advice such as the following: 'You may be able to get help with the cost of travel to visit someone (!) in prison. To get help you must be visiting your partner or a close relative like your son or daughter, or your mother or father.' Then in smaller letters: 'We use partner to mean a person you are married to or a person you live with as if you are married to them.' Apart from reminding me of a rude story beginning 'My father makes counterfeit money, my mother brews synthetic gin, my sister sells kisses to sailors', this advice leads me to look afresh at the word 'partner', which I always associated with respectable solicitors, accountants and other sorts of businessmen. Now it has a positively filthy ring.

This fascinating form deserves closer attention, so I'm going to leave it on the kitchen table on top of an orderly pile, and when the household chaos gets out of hand I shall apply myself to its carefully structured pottiness and cheer myself up.

# July

# I remember it well

I'm losing my grip: I just mixed the stuffing for the pork with a teaspoon instead of a fork. I've never done that before in my life. Before I know where I am I'll be walking on the cracks between the paving stones and eating apples in random bites instead of all round the middle, then the top, then the bottom. I might even start buttering toast with the straight-bladed knives rather than the ones with a sort of back-leaning curve. I regard it as a bad omen if, reaching blindly into the knife basket, I take hold of a straight-bladed one – so I cheat and look at it through half-closed eyes. It is also a bad omen if, taking hold of the lipstick, I find myself with the business end in the left rather than the right hand. If I abandon all these time-sanctified devices what will happen to the structure of my existence – let alone the misfortune which might attend such laxity? Oh help.

I have been thinking a lot about structure. When you're trying to write a play you have to. Novels are bad enough, but if, when you have assembled your characters on stage, you find you've forgotten to give one of them anything to say, you have to start again. You cannot leave a highly paid and sensitive actor sitting in a corner, speechless, like a beef olive. Unless, of course, you are sufficiently quick-witted to claim that you meant to do it – that it is highly significant, and a paradigm of the parameters of meaning, communication and alienation: a symbolic rendering of the essential *isness* of being – or some such tripe. In the end it's easier simply to extract the character. I *hate* plays I can't understand, no matter how inspired the direction or superb the lighting, and not being able to understand your own play is a nightmare of annoyance. A nice neat beginning, middle and end is what's called for. Life itself being such a frantic mess, with loose ends flying randomly all over the place, we need order *somewhere*.

History is another rich source of frustration, since it is impossible to go back and check on the facts. If you have an argument with somebody about the precise whereabouts of Ulan Bator you can always go and have a look, but the past swallows up truth like a bulldog and you cannot get its jaws open. Take Beryl, the jam sandwiches and the newspaper. Beryl's daughter remembers with vivid clarity that she was, at least once, sent to school with her jam sandwiches wrapped up in newspaper, and Beryl *knows* that she wasn't. She knows this with absolute certainty, like she knows the sun rose yesterday (she isn't absolutely certain it will rise tomorrow), and Rudi knows the opposite with the same conviction. What is truth?

When I was a little girl I saw a Green Man in Edgbaston. I can see him now, made of leaves in the form of a person, one leg forward, half-running because he was being mobbed by little boys. I don't think my mother would agree that I saw this figure. But I did. Beryl says gloomily that all this augurs ill for biography. I think she's right and we should all commit our own versions of events to print before some clown starts speculating on the exact nature of our relationship with our bank manager. I can think of nothing more maddening than having people talking about you, and being dead. My own daughter came in last night, coiffure on end, and announced that she'd just passed a derelict church where devil-worshippers were holding a Black Mass. She said she'd heard wolves howling and horrible unearthly satanic screechings. She is perhaps fortunate in her mother, for I see no reason to doubt her. These misguided people were probably trying to impose their own type of structure on the muddle of life.

I'm going to make a gooseberry fool in a minute and I will be very careful not to stir it widdershins. And I shall use a wooden spoon because in the past I always have, and if anyone says he remembers me using a fork I shall thump him.

## Sixties' child

I saw Katherine Whitehorn and Peregrine Worsthorne at the *Spectator* party, but I didn't get to talk to either of them: which is probably just as well, since if I'd been aware of the views they were each to express in their Sunday columns I would have bored them to death by agreeing with them. Nothing is less conducive to lively debate than breathless gasps of 'Oh, you're so *right*'. Child abuse was their subject, and very sound they both were. As Katherine Whitehorn observed, 'We see the family as a bulwark against the world and need to believe a lot of charming things about it – including quite a few that ain't so.'

It may sound a trifle strange, coming from the home front, but I have always entertained serious doubts about the family. Most of my friends could hardly wait to get out of the ones they were born into and run their own on more open lines – if indeed they hold on to them at all. It is to their friends that my generation turns when it feels in need of comfort or support. Many of our children still live with us – largely, I suppose, for financial reasons – and the only possible policy is: front door wide open and individual bedroom doors firmly shut, plenty of merry general chat and the minimum of intimate questioning, friends welcome at all times. Luckily the house is large enough for the less gregarious to closet themselves alone when it becomes necessary, and I, at least, have little sense of the stifling familial claustrophobia usual in my childhood. I will never forget the lowering of spirits when, out to tea with my little friends, their daddy came home from work and the fun was over. 'Sssh! Mr Montreal is going to read his newspaper now and you must all be quiet.' It may have been then that I began to consider the wisdom of those tribes, which keep the men in one long house and the women and children in another. I'm sure (I think) that Mr Montreal did not abuse his children, but they were not compatible. Daddies are freer and easier these days, but something has clearly gone insanely wrong.

As far as I know, I've only met one woman who was abused as a child. She had kept herself precariously together all her life – had married and had children – and then her husband left her and she cracked. She talked for a while about her husband's defection, but it was her father who had destroyed her and there was nothing that could mend her. She talked about it endlessly, repetitively, her mind going round like a rat in a barrel, and there seemed no hope of release. We asked her if she'd told her husband and she turned on us with contempt: if she'd done that he would have said that *now* he knew what was wrong with her and why she was as she was, and would have left her even sooner. She said her mother had known what was happening but had refused to do or say anything. The responsibility for keeping the family together lay with her and she had to be silent. Her father was a popular, outgoing sort of person, with brightly coloured ties, and a watch with a chain, and she couldn't shame him in the eyes of the community. I cannot tell you what I wistfully hoped would happen to that man.

For the present increase in incest Peregrine Worsthorne blames the Sixties, and I agree with him. When the Western world sat up and said 'Cor, sex is jolly, let no holds be barred', any idiot could have foreseen what would happen. For years already, well-meaning counsellors had been warning us that if we harboured a secret fantasy within our bosoms – say, of crucifying an aardvark on a lilac bush to the sound of violins – we must not be ashamed, for many other people, similarly repressed, shared our fantasy and, if we would but express it, we could form a group and send out a newsletter and not be lonely any more. The unspeakable, once spoken, takes on actuality, becomes possible in reality, and the devil is out of his den. How the meaning and purpose of taboo was so swiftly and completely lost sight of is a mystery, how proscriptions so powerful could be suddenly disregarded beyond understanding. The climate of opinion is responsible, I suppose. But how and why did it begin? It must be put down in the end to human arrogance, to the view that our instincts (which form taboos) ally us only to the brute creation, and we should use our reason to tell us how to behave. Unfortunately the baser instincts, which the taboos held in check, are even more powerful, so reason is perverted to justify them. Sometimes I really hate the human race.

Peregrine Worsthorne writes that once, over lunch, a foreigner remarked that he was thinking of going to bed with his daughter, and had *he*, Worsthorne, considered going to bed with his? It is sad and bad and mad, and the imagination boggles, but I do rather wish I could have seen Perry's face.

# Crumbling urns

I'm going to talk about the weather. I haven't talked about anything else for days now. There doesn't really seem to *be* anything else. Our friend Hylan just flew in from New York, rather looking forward to the cool of an English summer, but was disconcerted when, having descended through one layer of cloud into an area of blue, he saw below him another layer of cloud. With this two-ply effect no wonder all our days have turned green. We used to have an urn in the middle of the garden. It contained a bit of lavender and some Ragged Robin, and acted as a receptacle for a number of windborne weed seeds of one sort and another. Even small trees had hopefully attempted to take root in it. The other morning after a night of relentless rain it abandoned hope, purpose and function and simply fell apart. Hylan surveyed it sympathetically and remarked that he could see how it had felt. Gazing at it afresh, from this point of view, I was overwhelmed by a sense of empathy. Everything had got too much for it and it had quietly given up. It hadn't exactly committed suicide but it had, as it were, turned its face to the wall. Now we have all those orphaned weeds and infant trees to dispose of as well as its shattered remains. How do you dispose of an urn?

Wringing the rain out of my hair recently I considered travelling abroad in search of the sun. As far as I can gather, it's blazing down too much everywhere except here. Everywhere else people are sick of it and praying for our rain. Hylan says England's future lies in becoming a theme park: a rain theme park – and tourists will come from all over the world to see what it's like. Rain forests will spring up from the urns in our gardens and the seas will lap at our doorsteps. Already the gulls are here, their cries vying with the burglar alarms (Alfie says the local wives turn on the burglar alarms to alert their husbands that it's time for lunch), and the pavements resemble beaches as the sewers overflow in the gutters. *But* travel involves – well, travelling – and I'm not sure I wouldn't rather get wet. The daughter set off with her friend Anna last week: destination Italy. On the salient documents, every time it was appropriate to mention the point of departure the word Heathrow was writ large, but when they got there the airport staff said that that flight flew from Gatwick. They rang Gatwick to enquire if the flight was, by any chance, running late, in which case the little girls could hasten over there. And, of course, it was the only single flight in the country which was running on time. So they had to fly to Bologna via Paris. We had sent them by registered post – Janet signed them in and Anna's sister had to sign them out the other end – so we knew they were safe enough, but I used up a whole day sitting by the phone, gibbering. It takes it out of one. The car had also sustained a puncture on the way to the airport, and all in all the hazards of getting from hither to yon may outweigh the tedium of sitting watching the trees dripping.

I did arrange in one week to travel to Nantes, Builth Wells and the Isle of Wight. Unfortunately I wasn't thinking at the time; I did not consult the diary or wall chart, and discovered that I had agreed to be in all those places more or less simultaneously. It is difficult enough to get to anywhere even with your wits about you, passport in hand and your itinerary laid out, but my plans were clearly ridiculous. In the meantime I had also arranged to do several things (including a bit of work) in London, and had completely forgotten about everything else. Usually, at this time, London is deserted except for people from other countries who have come here to refresh themselves in the rain. Now that the airports refuse to relinquish the indigenous population in search of the sun we're *all* here, inviting each other to parties, barbecues, weddings and similarly ill-considered ventures. There are obviously too many of us, since even with the airports and prisons insanitarily overcrowded there are still plenty of us left on the streets or entertaining in our homes. Space travel must be the only answer. It has always annoyed me that the conception of tele-transportation has never borne fruit. If, instead of schlepping about with all that luggage, we could merely be dematerialised and reconstituted in a more salubrious environment, then I would not complain. Transgressors could be whisked off to Mars and those of us who had in the past elected to go to Benidorm could, instead, go to Venus. Our football hooligans could fling their beer cans into infinity, and our little children could be taken to the theme park of the Milky Way. The only trouble is that, if we are to believe the astronomers, the climate on our neighbouring planets is even worse than it is here. I can hardly believe it. I think our poor urn was aspiring in a microcosmic way to the condition of a Black Hole, a White Dwarf or a Collapsar. Good luck to it.

# Enchanting Welshmen

I have always had a great fondness for the Village Show. It brings tears to my eyes, representing, as it does, months and weeks and hours and hours of loving and laborious enterprise. The cakes and confections, all with a slice cut out to reveal the texture, are more moving than, say, the works of Henry Moore, the tea-cosies with their appliquéd pigs and bunnies more immediately human than the paintings of Picasso. I'm not so keen on the flower arrangements, which tend to the surrealistic, but the beans and the carrots and the radishes meticulously presented in small artistic groups are positively cathartic. This is probably because, if you know anything of the background to these vegetables, pity and horror are appropriate responses. The passions which animate those who grow them are far deeper and more violent than anything experienced by your Royal Academician. Rivalry, envy, suspicion and skulduggery are rife amongst their creators. Men with shotguns have frequently sat up all night for weeks on end to deter jealous competitors from introducing paraquat to their leek and onion beds, and many a woman has made and discarded a few gallons of jam before being entirely satisfied with the set and colour of her preserve.

The agricultural show is a larger version of the village show, with farm animals and pets and machinery; and the

royal Welsh Show is the largest of them all. We went to it last week and were told by several people that it was the largest show of its kind in Europe. I can believe it. It's a splendid occasion. It didn't even rain the day we were there. There were clouds around certainly, crouching above the adjacent hills like hostile tribesmen, but they didn't attack. What's more, as far as we could tell, they were the only inimical element present since, as the show *is* so large, the inevitable rivalries were not so apparent. The sense of internecine strife noticeable in small communities was greatly diluted, and there was an air of carefree good fellowship. Janet did wonder briefly what would happen if a horsefly should bite just one of the glamorously groomed cows in the cattle-shed and set off a chain reaction, and some of the ponies were uncommonly mettlesome, but all was well. Our host from the Beeb, Iwan Thomas, took us on a tour of the beasts and the vegetables and the pies and jams and cushion-covers and lawn-mowers, and when we tired he hailed a BBC buggy and we toured in comfort to some merry jeering from passers by. It beat sitting in London with the waters rising, I can tell you.

Iwan explained that the pleasant atmosphere was due to the *mix*. There were country people and town people, South Welsh and North Welsh, peasants and bonheddi-gion, and even a few English. I'd have thought that that could prove explosive, but happily it was not the case. The hospitality had something to do with our feeling of well-being as we tottered from the BBC building to the HTV one and back again. Sitting with a glass of beer and a fag, I observed Sir Geraint Evans approaching, and compelled by consideration for the glorious tonsils was about to douse the latter in the former when I noticed that he was the only other person in the vicinity who was also clutching a fag: life is full of surprises. We met a gentleman from HTV who was born and brought up in the village adjacent to our country cottage and whose best friend is the local gamekeeper. Little tiny world, made even smaller by telly. I have never willingly watched a game of cricket in my life but the day after our outing I turned on the match at Headingly because the commentator was Tony Lewis and he had been the gentleman on my left at dinner. I could listen to him talking for a very long time – even about silly mid-offs. I seldom really enjoy dinner parties but I had to be dragged away from this one. I think the success of the dinner was also due to the mix. Our hostess, Teleri Bevan, had gathered together a group of enchanting Welshmen and I'd forgotten how they could talk. The ghosts of past Welshmen talk in my kitchen in the country in the small hours. I have never, so far, gone down to join them, but next time I will. I shall go to the village show and come back and tell them all about it – tactfully, of course, for their beans, carrots, sheep, cattle and dogs will doubtless have been infinitely superior to anything produced today.

# August

# Six legs bad

We woke the other morning to the unusual sight of sunlight streaming through the windows and rose early. As Someone was preparing the matutinal coffee he noticed that the electric kettle, which had been about to come to the boil, was now in retreat, slowly backing away from the moment when it would normally switch itself off. It just went off. And so did the fridge/freezer and everything else. We wondered whether we had been singled out for misfortune but the entire street was affected. We could tell, because for one thing, there were no burglar alarms clanging away. The cat had been sick in front of the Aga, so I put yesterday's newspaper over that and boiled a pan of water on my antique New World gas stove. I was about to pour it on to the tea bags when I noticed a dead wasp floating in it, so I had to throw it away and start again. I then saw another wasp lying on its stomach in a few grains of sugar on the marble slab so I put the kettle on it. The milk of human kindness had all ebbed away. Anyway I hate wasps. More than any other insect they seem to imagine they have a right to the space one had fancied was one's own: determinedly dipping their legs over the edge of one's glass into one's beer, sitting stupidly but spitefully in one's sandwich, or crawling in one's hair. I don't really regret squashing them. I just wish they wouldn't crunch. Boiling them is less traumatic, though doubtless no pleasanter for the wasp.

Then the fifth son reminded me that I had agreed to walk with him a mile or so to the camera shop and we set off. By now it was 10.30. A notice on the door said opening hours were between 9.30 and 6, but it lied. The place was barred, grilled, bolted and unquestionably shut. So we walked home again. Fortunately before I left I had remembered to tell Janet about what was concealed beneath the newspaper, but she did suggest that in future it might be advisable to put a notice on the site of the disaster in case I was too preoccupied to mention it and she might whisk up the paper without due care.

It *was* one of those days. A photographer came in the evening. By this time the electricity had been restored but I warned him that even when it was coursing round the cables our electricity was less than reliable. If the spindryer and the dishwasher are both in operation and somebody turns on the kettle everything goes off and we have to push a red button and start again. He said he was sure it would be all right. He'd once fused an aircraft carrier, but that was a single instance and things usually went well. So of course when he'd set up his reflecting things and his tripods and plugged in his lighting devices everything blew. It didn't seem to matter any more because we'd all gone limp. If I've learned anything in life it is that there is no point in making a fuss. When everything goes wrong I just wait patiently for somebody to fix it, and if they don't – well then they don't, and in the end it doesn't matter. This time the eldest son mended the fuse. There are certain things I don't do. I don't do fuses or tap washers or make speeches or go for complicated trips on public transport or cope with cat sick. There is no point in unnecessarily subjecting oneself to frustration, fright, confusion or nausea. Let George do it. On the other hand I am uncommonly brave when it comes to spiders. I don't like them, but I don't not like them nearly as much as Janet doesn't. The bargain is quite fair. She copes with the cats' digestive upsets and I handle the arachnids. If she is faced with a fully clad prawn I peel it for her, since her phobia extends to crustaceans. She can't abide things with more than the usual complement of arms and legs whereas I can take them in my stride.

I'm going to have to do something about the wasps though. I think there must be a colony of them nesting in the ivy, regarding the house and garden as their own. I don't want them committing suicide in the soup or letting themselves be eaten by the cats, and I don't fancy the idea of cyanide. Perhaps there's some way of electrocuting them. Another one has just foundered in the fifth son's last cup of tea before he leaves for his hols. Perhaps we could entice them into a hold-all and send them to an airport.

PS: There are two more dog-paddling in the sink and two have drowned.

# Plumbing the depths

The sink is blocked and the dishwasher is overflowing. I suspect in some dim region of my mind that in some dim region where the plumbing occurs these events are not unconnected. I hate paddling on the kitchen floor, but even more do I detest peeping into the intricacies of the plumbing. It just ought to work. Like one's liver. I'm rather vague as to what it's for and I've got no idea where it is. I just hope it's quietly fulfilling its purpose.

The same goes for motor cars. Some people like fiddling in their interiors, but most of us want them to work without hassle and get us to where we're going and back. And I don't like watches that don't work (I've got several of those) and most of all I don't like vacuum cleaners that don't work. I can never believe they couldn't do it if they tried, if they would just summon up some energy and will power they could easily suck up that dead moth with as much vigour as they were invented with. My past is littered with failed vacuum cleaners, and I often wish I hadn't given away my trusty Ewbank, which was a primitive sort of carpet sweeper with no vulnerable engine, only mechanically operated rotating brushes. But then, of course, there's the rub. The more sophisticated the machinery the likelier it is to be afflicted by some arcane ailment, and only people with degrees in its manner of being will be able to fix it.

Take the telephone. Sometimes it will work and sometimes it won't. Sometimes it rings and the person on the other end will say aggrievedly that they've been trying to get hold of us all day and where have we been, for God's sake? As there is always and invariably somebody in this house there is clearly here a failure in communication. It sounds to *them* as though it's ringing throughout the house, but here the silence is unbroken, except, of course, for the steady swish of water from the dishwasher. Only an expert in the ways of telephones can remedy this defect and often the experts have better fish to fry – worse, more glamorous types of malfunctioning than a misplaced ring.

The same thing happened at the office last week when the electricity was cut off without warning. The telephones stopped ringing and all their little lights went out. This caused confusion on several levels, with some of us holding that the telephone was dependent on the electricity supply and some holding that it wasn't. I pointed out that back at the house, where everything else had gone silent and dark, the telephone was working as well as it ever was: not marvellously, but consenting spasmodically to relay messages from one person to another as it should in the nature of its constitution. I remember old electricity cuts when the gas boiler had ceased to work because it was dependent on electricity to prime the pump or spark the dynamo or do something that gas can't do by itself. I thought it must be something like that. All over the country people were ringing the office and getting indignant at hearing a perfectly healthy ringing tone and no human response. They assumed that everyone had gone insouciantly off on holiday, and banged down their handsets with a muttered 'Tush'. This isn't good for the business image.

Now I'm going to get the mop and bucket and a lot of old newspapers and soak up the dishwater which has mostly gone under the fridge. I once had a vacuum cleaner that was supposed to suck up water: it didn't work. And then I'm not going to work for a week. I'm going away with a friend in a motor car away from all this nonsense. I'd feel safer if it was a horse and cart, but I'll simply keep my fingers crossed – as useful a ploy as any when it comes to machinery.

# Frites with everything

I was sitting on a boat the other day, wondering about the wisdom of this and debating with myself the proposition 'Abroad is bloody etc.' when I heard the voice of a compatriot raised in anger. 'When the cup is cracked', he was informing the world, 'in the crack lurks the virus hepatitis B. When the vessel is washed the washing process does not extend to the crack.' His child spoke: 'But Father', it said – rather spitefully, I thought, for clearly his papa had gone to all the trouble of sending him to public school – 'at school *everything's* cracked.' There was a short pause while papa thought round this one. At last he observed that it wasn't so important in a community: it was the hepatitis B of strangers that was so threatening. He may have been a doctor, or perhaps he'd failed at something. Whatever the cause, he was quite the most shaming chucker-about-of-weight on the boat.

This scare had all come about because his elder child had brought his mama tea in a cracked cup. 'Take that back at once,' his father had roared. 'Look after your mother.' The unfortunate youth who had inherited his father's charm had been told by the man behind the counter to go and do the other thing, and father had taken up the cudgels. Before you could blink he was behind the counter doing his weight-throwing, and the purveyor of tea in a cracked cup had been forced into a stance of crackissimus!

'At school everything's cracked'

mulish, total obstinacy – as well he might. We didn't blame him at all, cracked cup or no. Then our compatriot strode off. 'Ow gawd', we said to each other, 'he's gone to get the captain, and the ship will founder because nobody will be watching where it's going.' Sure enough, he came back with a person in an official jacket, but I think it was only the head steward. The head steward then brought another cup of tea, carrying it in a fashion rejected by hygiene experts, i.e. not by the handle, or on a saucer, but gripped round the rim by the fingers. He plonked it down before our compatriot, who said in his customary bellow that it was for his *wife*. But the crew had gone into hiding by that time. I know something about what happens to people who complain about the food because I know some people who've worked behind the scenes. The chef will indeed amend the rejected dish – in several ways, one of which is by spitting in it. If you have a complaint, make it and *leave*.

When we stopped for some *frites* and sausage on the other side it was quite relaxing to observe the proprietor of the lay-by stall idly scratching his armpit while hollowing out a bit of baguette to contain the sausage. In the shade lay an alsatian thoughtfully washing his – well, never mind what he was washing – and on the ground nearby lay windfalls from an apple tree. A contingent of local youth came speeding up in motor cars and rolled out drunk, and we consciously appreciated the foreignness of it all. Drunken French youth is subtly different from drunken English youth. More cheerful and a lot more friendly.

I'm busy trying to remember some French. I have a nightmare about getting into conversation with a local who will ask me what I do and I'll say I'm an *écrevisse* – or maybe an *escritoire*. Still, I was pleased yesterday when I saw a board outside a *café* advertising '100 'dwiches' – it only took me a minute or so to figure it out. And I've bought some wonderful postcards for people who annoy me. They feature a photograph of an intensely sensitive looking billy goat and are headed *Un intellectuel de gauche*. Sweet.

# French polish

Well, here we are again, back in Camden Town, and nothing has changed at all except that there are more and bigger holes in the road. These have men in them and so, I suppose, must be intentional. The roads around the holes are ankle deep in litter whereas the roads in Brittany were remarkably clear except for dog mess and I have had to revise my opinions of our respective nations. I was brought up to believe that compared with us all foreigners were uncleanly in their habits and unkind to animals, and you couldn't drink the water. I was also led to believe that the French had an innate sense of style and *chic* and, even clad in an old pillow case, by dint of slinging a belt of Toledo leather round the hips would draw all eyes. This is no longer so. Now they wear long shorts – one leg in tartan and the other in abstract shapes in day-glo colours. *Everybody* wears them in Quiberon: and peaked caps in the same mode. And *everybody* has a dog – either the small ridiculous sort or the big nasty (very nasty) sort. Yorkshire terriers seem to be the most favoured, followed by chihuahuas, followed by poodles, while the big ones are built on wolf lines and have a tendency to designer foam around the muzzle. Their owners absolutely dote on them

'C'est l'amour'

and the little ones get carried a lot of the time in bicycle baskets and handbags, and they are unusually happy. You can always tell. Camden dogs look morose by contrast. Perhaps it's because they have to pick their way around the litter in order to find a space for lavatorial purposes. We are a filthy lot.

One day we went to Carnac to look at what my friend Pat refers to as the 'mogoliths'. She was tired out with driving when she coined this term, but I find it excellently descriptive. She was as much impressed by the absence of drifting garbage as she was by the standing stones. If they were ours we'd have written our names and intimations of our libidinous preoccupations on them, and obscured them in empty crisp packets. I got very ratty wondering what they were for. What people would have gone to all the trouble of lining up those colossal boulders for as far as the eye could see, and why would they bother? All those broken fingernails, crushed toes and pulled muscles. How much of each boulder is buried in the earth and where did they get them from? What's it all about? People keep telling me they're for esoteric astronomical calculations and from them you could figure out when there was going to be an eclipse, but that seems to me a very frivolous explanation. I don't give a monkey's when there's going to be an eclipse. Does anybody? Did they? Eclipses, after all, are not a daily occurrence and I can think of an almost infinite number of things to worry about more. Maybe they were planning a Channel tunnel and then wisely thought better of it and planted the stones so the kiddies could run in straight lines in the school sports. Maybe they're the then equivalent of motorway cones.

Another theory suggests that they have mystical properties, so Pat and I rested our foreheads on one to check this out and see if we got any prehistorical vibes. A passing Frenchman, seeing us thus engaged, observed to his companion, '*Ah, la communication avec les roches*', as though he'd have expected nothing else from two nutty English *dames*. We gave quite a lot of simple pleasure to several foreigners with our incomplete command of the language and our efforts to put up a tent. I say 'our', but I really mean Pat and the girls: I sat that one out. The whole business looked quite as esoteric as any astronomical problem. There were some Germans watching too, helpless with teutonic mirth, because at one point the thing was going up inside out. I rather wanted to go and ask them who'd won the war, but that would have led to an unseemly *fracas à l'Anglais*. Word would have got back and we'd have been castigated as hooligans, unworthy representatives of our country, incapable of keeping out of trouble. As it was, we behaved with notable decorum throughout. I didn't even drink or smoke – well, not a lot – and we ate hundreds of potatoes with butter, and *croissants* and *tartes*, and we kept on asking why Breton vegetables made ours taste like boiled sphagnum moss and why their fish was so fresh. I know they get them straight out of the water, but we're surrounded by the stuff and our fish doesn't taste like that. Even their lettuce tasted like lettuce, while ours doesn't taste of anything. You will ask why, if I don't like it here, I don't go and live abroad. And I respond – well, I would if I could afford it. So there.

It's just occurred to me that in a million years or so people will be wondering why we dug so many holes in the road, and I have the answer to the riddle of the standing stones. The Council put them up. It was undoubtedly a job opportunities scheme.

# September

# Hotel du lack

Staying in hotels is not what it used to be. It used to be quite straightforward. They'd give you a key and a lad would carry your Gladstone bag up the stairs to your room. If you required a glass of Madeira and a biscuit to sustain you, you rang a bell and the owner's wife sent up a lass with a tray. You flung up your window, or did whatever you do should it be the casement variety, and leaned out and inhaled the air that happened to be on offer according to where your hotel was located. This is so no longer. For a start, no one opens the front door for you, even in the larger (very large) establishments. The doors open Sesame all by themselves as you approach. Many doors in many types of buildings and trains do this now, and I always wonder what happens when the electricity fails, as it does from time to time. It does quite often in Camden, but apart from the darkness, the ruin of the freezer contents and the fact that nobody can blow-dry her hair, it doesn't matter all that much. I cannot, however, imagine one of our larger new hotels blundering along by candle-light with people on the inside trying to get out, and people on the outside conceivably trying to get in, through those electronically operated doors. People would have to walk up and down the stairs thoughtfully provided by the management in case of fire. Clearly they do not believe any lesser eventuality would induce people to stay out of the lifts. And I don't suppose the bedroom doors would respond to those dinky little cards which you slip in the lock in place of a key.

At the weekend I stayed on the fifth floor of a large modern hotel and it was pretty much the same as staying in a large modern hospital – the sort in which you visit those friends who have had the foresight to take out private medical insurance – and almost as dispiriting. 'Soulless', I think, is how one would choose first to describe it, and 'technologically confusing' next. Even the taps in the bathroom operated on a rather frenchified system previously unfamiliar to me, and if Alun Owen had not shown me where they conceal the thing to change the TV channel (in a stack of things opposite the TV) I should have gone mad with nothing to read but brochures extolling the hedonistic delights on offer in this and similar (identical actually, I daresay) hotels all over the place. I couldn't open the window to lean out and savour the view because it opened only the merest crack to discourage guests with a tendency to defenestration from indulging themselves. There can be nothing worse for a hotel's image than the wholesale suicide of dissatisfied clients. Not, I hasten to assure you, that the place was uncomfortable. It wasn't, but it wasn't *comfortable* either, if you see what I mean. It suggested the idea of a very expensive prostitute who does all the right things, as it were, but hasn't got her heart in it, and at a price. This image has occurred to me because, as the evening drew on and we sat in the bar (open plan, deep armchairs, as well as the sort that go with tables, *ersatz* flickering flames on top of a box and a swimming pool round somewhere), I noticed an elderly gent with a youngish woman who appeared to be very fond of him – tweaking his ageing

119

ears and patting his drooping cheek. 'How sweetly strange,' I said. 'I wonder why she loves him so,' and Alun, regarding me with some incredulity said, 'She's a hooker.' Why didn't I see that? Later that night (after a perfect stranger had suddenly elected to audition for us: it was that sort of night) my friend Jane was awakened by a frenzied banging on her door which nearly frightened her to death. She telephoned for assistance and Security was sent up (I see Security as having a slavering beast on a leash) but neglected to tell her whether they had apprehended anyone or what was going on. She rang back after a while and learned that a woman had been looking for somebody all over the sixth floor. I thought it probable that this woman was somebody with a better claim to the elderly gent than the lady who presently had him in her clutches, but we shall never know since she went out into the night through those mute and undiscriminating automatic doors. Another unexpressed human tragedy, but I wasn't all that moved because modern hotels are not conducive to great imaginative sympathy. Next time I'm going to try a boarding house and if the windows won't open I'll break them.

# Fundamental error

I'm glad our editor didn't like *The Last Temptation of Christ*. That is, I'm sorry he had to spend a boring few hours, for that is never pleasant, but I'm glad we're in accord. I'm also glad he appreciated Lenny the Lion, who is undoubtedly the funniest character in the whole thing. I fell asleep several times and wanted very much to go home, but my friend the ex-monk insisted that fair play called upon us to sit it out. As a result I disliked the film even more out of sheer resentment at its length.

The third son went to see it with Beryl the following night, fell asleep, woke himself up by snoring too loudly and left to go and have his dinner. I have often noticed that the young are more resolute than my own generation when it comes to the question of polite endurance. Then I saw Martin Scorsese on television saying something so flatulently fatuous that I stopped listening out of sheer annoyance. It was to the effect that mankind has concentrated too greatly on the spiritual side of Christ and neglected to appreciate his humanity, whereas I cannot remember the last time I heard a churchman speaking at length on the numinous aspects of Our Lord. I find it ironic that the fundamentalists should have been so vociferous in their protests, since fundamentalism is characterised by a clod-hopping literalness and so is the motivation behind this film. It goes something as follows – Jesus was a man: I am a man: I spend most of my time thinking about sex: ergo, Jesus spent most of his time thinking about sex. It is as daft as thinking 'I have a verruca: Jesus must have had a verruca', or 'I am frightened of spiders: I bet Jesus was absolutely terrified of the things'. The silly fellow who wrote the book was clearly a Manichee, for the film is preceded by some lines about his lifelong battle between the flesh and the spirit. The point is that the two should, by the Grace of God, co-exist comfortably, not scrap it out in a struggle to the death; and if Jesus didn't get it right then there's very little hope for the rest of us.

Millenium at M&S.

Does nobody remember any more that the love of God transcends sex as the sun transcends a bonfire? Yes, I know some people do, but they're keeping remarkably quiet about it. It isn't fashionable. This is a pity, for there is nothing in the world quite as interesting as the experiences of the saints. People's sexual problems pall on one. There is a banality about them: a claustrophobic circularity, and no light at the end of the tunnel – if you'll pardon the expression. Still, most of the work of the saints was done in obscurity, not on film, and we can only hope there are some of them out there still engaged in the continuing task of redemption.

I read recently that a member of the American 'rapture' cult has prophesied that the world will end this week, and the elect, living and dead, will be whisked off to Heaven, while the rest of us will be left here with the Anti-Christ to contend with, possibly condemned to watch the *Last Temptation* until the millennium comes about. I see myself in Marks & Spencer's with the sky rent overhead and one or two of my fellow shoppers disappearing through the roof, while there is mild disturbance in the local cemetery. The literal view is a form of insanity. God's ways are too subtle for us to comprehend. The glass is dark and there is very little use in our trying to project images on to it. We just have to wait until we are permitted to see, and many of us would be well advised to keep our mouths shut in the meantime. I'm going to myself in future. I can discuss politics with equanimity, but potty ideas about 'Gahd' drive me mad.

# A dusty answer

The man who mends the tumble-dryer wended his way through the clematis the other day and when he reached the laundry door, fending off the castor oil plant, he said, as I greeted him, 'Dr Livingstone, I presume.' I explained that the tumble-dryer had been incapacitated by a brassière hook which had caught in its metal perforations and tied the other clothes into a knot. For some reason this had caused all the machines in the basement to give people electric shocks when they touched them – a sort of contagious hysteria – and everyday existence had assumed a dangerous aspect. He said that was nothing. Last time he'd had to treat a tumble-dryer with this complaint it had brought about a divorce. A steel reinforced brassière had become detached from its cantilever which had gone through the barrel part to foul the engine. The housewife said, as he retrieved, and triumphantly displayed it, that she herself personally never wore that sort of bra and she'd have to have a word with her husband when he got home. That, however, is not the point. The point is that I was recently surprised to find the home described in an article as a 'dream house', 'Everything is just too perfect'. This is, of course, hugely gratifying, but I do wonder whose house the author of the piece was visiting under the impression that it was ours. He says there seems little to disturb the flow of life. What can he *mean*? He says there is 'just enough mess to reassure those visitors who mistakenly believe they have wandered into a Sunday colour supplement feature'. *Pardon?* What standards can he be judging us by? What was he drinking? Whatever it was I could do with some if that's the effect it has.

Another lady asked last week how I would choose to describe the house. 'Elegant?' she suggested (she has not actually been here) I thought for a while and said 'dusty' might more exactly convey the *ambience*. While Janet was on her hols the cat was sick on a pile of clean washing that she had left. Nobody was prepared to deal with this emergency so I tried to persuade the eldest son that it was his cat, Cadders, who had perpetrated the outrage. Unfortunately we all know that it is my cat, Puss, who can't hold her Kit-E-Kat, so I had to fall back on pathos and remind him that it was my birthday and I couldn't be expected to cope with anything too demanding. He was very noble about it and did what was necessary but I don't think people in the supplement features are often discommoded in this fashion. I don't think they lose their marriage lines or everybody's birth certificates, or the important papers their mother gave them to look after. And I don't believe their kettles electrocute them when they propose to make a cup of tea. And I do believe they can actually walk into most of their rooms. Some of ours are piled so high with old papers and schoolbooks and broken pictures that you can't even put a coffee mug down on the floor. I do mean, sincerely, to tidy it all up one day, just as I mean to learn to dot i's properly. At present whenever I dot an i I get it on the up-stroke of the next letter so you can't see it and I have to do it twice ('twice' is all right because the next letter is lower than the i – oh God, I wish life wasn't so complicated).

The man who mends the tumble-dryer just rang to say

the reason he hadn't been back was because of the postal strike. The spare part has been held up somewhere. He said it wasn't that they ever used the post. They use Securicor who are now so busy that they have a backlog and do not know when they will be able to deliver the spare part, and I only hope the cat is feeling better because washing has to be dried and I don't trust the tumble dryer in its present incomplete stage. There are enough shocks in life reading about your own home life from a strange point of view.

# Not so funny

Humour is a peculiar thing. I have never been able to understand why Charlie Chaplin, Laurel and Hardy, and the rest are considered *funny*. Some of the things they do are quite clever, but I sit staring at the TV screen seeing no cause at all to so much as smile, and wishing they'd put on the ads with Roy Kinnear in them. Because he was wonderfully funny apparently without trying. Should anything with Norman Wisdom in it announce itself I fly to change the channel – even if it's only for darts or Dynasty – since he is acutely embarrassing and, as far as I'm concerned, embarrassment is the opposite of humour. Except for *Fawlty Towers* which is almost funnier than anything. How confusing. The other day a man said to me, 'The harpist's arrived – unfortunately', and I don't know why, but I laughed for hours. (I can't be bothered to go into details but circumstances demanded one, and she had.) Then Beryl rang up to say that life reminded her of those pot plants that you keep for ages; and their lower leaves shrivel and then their upper leaves, and you keep on watering them... I thought she was going to say 'and then suddenly they put out a little bud and it blossoms', but she didn't. She said, 'And then you throw them away.' I found this vastly more cheering than the expected tiresomely hopeful bud.

There's an anthology of 'comedy classics' on the drawing-room table. I think I must have bought it myself in a moment of despair as a stocking-filler for one of the children. I almost remember doing so and I can't think of any other reason why it should be there next to Ford Madox Ford and Colette – who are there because I read them in another moment of despair and couldn't be bothered to put them back on the shelves. In yet another such moment I began to read this anthology and found my spirits instantly lifted by a remark from Richard Gordon's *Special Delivery* to the effect that midwifery is a subject 'which usually produces a sharp reactionary attack of misogyny in its students'. I knew that it did because a trainee doctor had told me so and I had felt sympathetic despite being about to give birth to somebody or other. I could see exactly how the whole business could easily pall on one after a very short while. I quite understand Richard Gordon's Lamont who had 'been so moved by his experiences he was on the point of breaking off his engagement. "The frightful women... I can't understand that anyone would ever want to sleep with them. That someone obviously has done so in the near past is quite beyond me".' When I was really fed up with childbearing – i.e. when I was in the throes of it and just remembering how painful, uncomfortable and simply humiliating it

'Ve haf vays of making you laugh

could be – people were wont to say it was all perfectly natural, and a lot of people also held that it was very beautiful. I don't know what their criteria were, but I could never see it myself. I find Lamont much more understandable and reassuring.

You could trust a doctor who spoke his mind like that. I suppose humour is something to do with truth and little to do with high-flown sentiments. I still can't see why it's got anything to do with big shoes and a bowler hat or breaking plates, and custard pies, but then there's a lot I don't understand about other people and what makes them laugh is some of it. Half the nation used to roar at *ITMA* when I was a child and I never could see why. I quite enjoyed it but it didn't make me laugh. Then along came *Take It From Here* and that did, whereas my mother rather disapproved of it and couldn't understand what I was falling off the chair about. It *is* odd. The same things make people cry, and indeed much the same things make people happy. The area of disagreement lies not only in politics, religion, race, but in what you find funny. I hope it doesn't occur to anyone to go to war about it.

# October

# Escape route

I have often thought that life is very like a party (I write this because I keep hearing vicar-type people making similar remarks on the wireless and the style is catching) and we who live are like party-goers. Some of us enjoying every minute and meeting interesting new people, and some of us gazing round dementedly for ways out. The principal door is frequently blocked by people arriving and your host is often adjacent to it, perhaps checking that no one leaves too soon. You start fantasising about crawling out on your hands and knees, unrecognisable by virtue of the ice bucket you have had the foresight to put your head in, or leaping out of the window of the ladies' lav hoping you were correct in your assumption that the party is taking place on the ground floor. You note with increasing malice the man with the saxophone and wonder if you would ever regain your good name if you shoved an avocado down the bit the noise comes out of. You wonder what would happen if you poured a bottle of white wine over the man plugged into the electric piano – or whatever the damnable thing is; and you wonder what on earth you're doing there in the first place. Most of all you wonder why they play so loudly. People are meant to converse at parties but there really isn't any point if you can't even hear yourself think. I suppose the musicians see it differently: they are for making a noise; it is their task and their *raison d'être*, and make a noise they will, come hell or high water.

I was talking to – or rather howling at – an estate agent at a party the other day. Estate agents come exceedingly low on my list of desirable acquaintances. I prefer undertakers who perform a similar, though more permanent, function and tend not to gazump you; but you don't often meet undertakers at parties, unless of course it's somebody's last one. Where was I? Oh yes, I was talking to this estate agent and he was more entertaining than most in that he regretted that you couldn't eat dry rot. He held it would be some sort of consolation if you could fry the fungus in your omelettes while your house sank around you. I agreed with him. Then I met a lady who was grieved because a friend of hers had got divorced and was reduced to living alone in the country with the dog. I said it sounded all right to me, and the lady looked as though she found me unbalanced. Then I met another lady who said the only way she'd made her marriage work was by stabling her husband in the Home Counties while she lived in London. I mentioned this to Janet who said thoughtfully that it was probably the best idea – you could meet him once on Sunday in the months with an R in them and that would keep the romance alive. People do differ so in their views. Once upon a time it was common to pray for the grace of an early death whereas it is now more fashionable to attempt to live forever; although I do know one or two people who plan to have stamped on their foreheads, in case of accident, the words 'Over 60. Kindly do not resuscitate'. However, this is unusual and generally regarded as somehow ungrateful. You mean you're not *enjoying* this lovely party?

My view is that if Heaven's all it's cracked up to be you'd

be insane not to want to make the change. I can't remember what the pavements are said to be made of – chrysalite and beryl or something – but I'm quite sure they're not being constantly dug up so the gas men can put in new pipes, closely followed by electric men, water men, telephone men and men who are employed by the council to slap down new designer paving stones, simply for the hell of it. Our street at present bears all the appearance of an open grave. As far as I remember only St Michael the Archangel, has any form of transport, so there won't be any parking problems. I'm a bit doubtful about those choirs but I'm sure they'll have the consideration to keep down the decibel level. It was perfectly wonderful to leave the party of which I have been speaking and step out into the silent night.

# Designs on the young

I wonder what this means: 'The Owner will at the request and expense of the Purchaser execute all such further instruments as the Purchaser may require for the purpose of confirming the Purchaser's title to...' It's in English I suppose but I don't understand a word of it. Ever since the post returned I have received only nasty boring mail couched in terms I cannot comprehend. I inadvertently overpaid the taxman some months ago and have just heard that he might hand back the money I 'allegedly' gave him when he's looked into the details. What does he mean 'allegedly'? How insulting. The most annoying communication of all is an appeal from a school to which the daughter briefly went until we realised she'd be better off in the monkey house in the zoo. This school has a great reputation, so I think we may have chanced upon it in a bad moment. At all events the teachers we encountered distinguished themselves by recommending some American porn for teenagers as further reading for the child, and refusing to discuss the little matter of the girl with the knife because she was in another form. She came – they said loftily – from a deprived background, and further they would not go. If – they said – we were not satisfied perhaps we would care to try another educational establishment. So we did and it's perfectly fine: no Mac the Knife and no nymphets and no appeals for half your kingdom. The previous school is seeking to extend its facilities for Music, Fine Arts, Textiles, Design and Technology. Whatever happened to reading, writing and arithmetic? These tiresome subjects were conspicuous by their absence in our short acquaintance with the place and while I would not give a penny to it even in the interests of education, I certainly am not going to fund their designs and technology which in my opinion would be better served in an Institute of Higher Education to which the young should go, having mastered the basic skills. The enclosed leaflet helpfully suggests the means by which one could relieve oneself of considerable sums – 'either a lump sum or a monthly payment' or 'a covenant' with an initial load of money and then a bit over four years. All mysterious stuff catered for by the forms thoughtfully included. The way I feel about forms I can't cope with them even when there's money in it for *me*. They quote some wheeze whereby the money you pay goes against tax. I don't understand it but the leaflet poses the question

'How often does the Inland Revenue contribute to your children's welfare?' Well, not a lot, but so what?

I recently bought a book published in the twenties called *Handicraft in the School*, which treats these matters as peripheral rather than central, suggesting, for example, that *Radiation* should be studied, being 'such a universal law of nature. All lines should be made to fine off at their points to emphasise their exhaustion.' Then to Greek vases, Venetian glass and the subject of compound curves. 'Shell forms supply many beautiful shapes, and soft felt hats, Panama hats, girls' or ladies' hats, oilskin hats, umbrellas (open and shut), birds' feathers, and things of

STILL LIFE
WITH HAT

that description indicate other suitable forms.' At this point I wondered whether all teachers have always been slightly crazy but reminded myself that handicrafts was usually confined to Friday afternoons when the nitty-gritty of the week's work was left behind, and all that, in those days, was required of parents was the loan of their Greek vases, hats, umbrellas and any old feathers they might chance to have lying around. The kiddies would leave school more or less literate and fitted for employment. Then in the evenings they could draw ladies' hats for relaxation. Which is as it should be. If everyone is encouraged to take up music, design and fine arts as a way of life, who's going to man the trains? I asked the daughter if she was taught to cook or fill out forms – never mind maths and Shakespeare etc. – and she says she can't remember. I rest my case.


# Sheep shock


I put the cow creamer in the dishwasher the other day. It reposed there belly upwards with its legs sticking out, bearing a striking though melancholy resemblance to some real cows I saw in a recent photograph. These animals had contracted a disease which first drove them mad and then killed them. The disease has a long name which I cannot remember in full and which must be new since, previously, I believe the affliction was confined in this country to sheep, and called 'scrapie'. Somewhere else it is called 'kuru', and human beings suffer from it. Once it was supposed that it resulted from cannibalism, and particularly from the consumption of human brains, but now it has been suggested that the unfortunate sufferers may merely have smeared themselves in blood. I read this in the newspapers, which never now tell the full story for fear of libelling somebody too insignificant to make it worth while, and so I do not know whether this blood is human or not. It seems a dumb thing to do anyway and must attract unwelcome clouds of flies. However, it is not nearly so dumb as giving cows sheep to eat. Dead old sheep, unfit for human consumption, have been minced up and translated into protein pellets to encourage cattle to grow bigger or supply more milk or maybe run faster or hurdle low fences. I don't really know the motive behind it. All I know is that whoever thought the idea up must himself have had very dodgy brains because now cows have contracted the sheep's disease.

I think of a nursery school. Teacher gazes meditatively round wondering what ideas the little blisters are hatching. 'No', she says, drawing a bow at a venture, 'we don't put plasticine in the fish tank – or pull Samantha's hair or take the hamster out for a walk.' She does not, unless she is herself deranged, say: 'We do not take the goldfish home in our hankie, or climb on the roof and jump down the chimney, or put the potting compost in Samantha's ears.' That is – some ideas do not occur to the normal mind, and I would have thought that feeding cattle on processed mutton was one of them. It would not strike the beef-eating public that it should request the meat producers not to muddle up the Sunday joints in this perverted fashion, until it learned of the *fait accompli*. It has now been admitted that human beings could contract this ovine/bovine disease by consuming contaminated meat. At first it was thought that only the cows' brains were a hazard, so some cows which had gone insane were slaughtered and beheaded, the rest of them duly turned into hamburgers etc. It is some time since I have bought sausages, meat pies, faggots or anything else unrecognisably chopped up because I heard of the wonderful new technology which can render every normally unpalatable and unacceptable part of the animal fit to be chewed and swallowed – even its bones and gristle – and if God had intended us to eat bones and gristle He would have given us different tastes and more efficient teeth. Now I am considering full vegetarianism on prudent, rather than humane, grounds. The only trouble being that the broadleaved veg may be radioactive, anything grown near London is full of lead, the merest lettuce may contain countless pesticides – likewise the fruit – and unless you boil the eggs for an hour or so you may get salmonella poisoning. Chickens are a fearful health hazard, the fish has probably died from swimming around in polluted waters, and the EEC wants to import all our wild game before it gets eaten in case it too is bearing some nameless scourge. I remember with nostalgia the time when all we had to worry about was trichinosis in the pork – although even then you could also get it from bear meat. Not a lot of people eat bear meat, but some who did did not live long enough to regret it. Maybe the bears had been eating pigs. It seems that in order to survive, unpoisoned, we should all simply grow our own bean sprouts on wet flannel. And I hate bean sprouts.

# Hawkers welcome

Two little girls knocked at the door the other day and asked if there were any odd jobs they could do to make money for some charity or other. They were *very* little girls and I shouldn't imagine they were terribly competent at anything yet. Anyway, so many odd jobs need doing that I couldn't think of any one in particular. I asked if they were travelling widely round Camden Town knocking on the doors of strangers and they said they were, so I asked if their mothers knew they were thus engaged and they said they did. I can only suppose that their mothers were unbelievably busy making chutney, and I don't know quite why but I also think they have left-wing tendencies. The little girls had privately-educated voices and nice clean frocks on and an air of informed good will, and were somehow subtly different from little conservatives. I didn't have long enough to question them further because they went off on the trail of good works, robbing me of the chance to explore further my theories as to the nature and behaviour of the young from families of varying political affiliations.

Then a man knocked at the door and said he was selling fitted carpets. He happened to have with him an acre or two of grey corded stuff and we happened to have several bedrooms in need, so we did a deal: on the spot, just like that. I'd been planning to do it for years and years and

'The knife-grinder... had a romantic air'

never got round to it. Normally it involves going to shops that sell carpet and making choices, and one simply hasn't got the time. It was very reasonably priced too – an important consideration, as often one simply hasn't got the money either. Being a carpet man he noticed with the acumen of his calling that the stairs were uncarpeted, as they have been for years since the last lot wore completely away. 'What about this then?' he enquired with a bright and encouraging glance, and I explained that I sincerely intended one day to do something about it, but not until I'd cleared out the loft and taken the contents down to the country. I said I just hadn't got the time to get round to it, so he said he'd empty the truck of carpet and do it for me. If he does he will have solved at a stroke a problem which has been dogging me for years. The untidiness of the loft has been a constant oppression and I have long suspected that moths and wasps build up colonies in there and then make forays downwards to ravage everything else in the place: or lie in wait to sting you, in the case of the wasps – and clog up the kitchen sink on some motiveless suicide mission.

Apart from little girls and the carpet man, people no longer call at the door offering their services. We are told to be wary if they do because they might, in fact, be after our savings; or they might be mad rapists or gangs of professional burglars who take everything, right down to the fridge – and, quite possibly, the carpets. It's years since I saw the man who used to come round to cane the chairs, and even longer since I saw the man who used to grind knives. Neither of them was particularly good at doing these things, but they gave the place a Dickensian, traditional feel as they sat incompetently amidst the tools of their trade, drinking tea and making conversation. The knife man had one leg and wore one ear-ring, and I always assumed he had been a seafarer. He had a romantic air, and although after his visits we frequently found a bottle of booze was missing I didn't really mind.

I wish the butcher and the baker still called, and the muffin man. Why not? It never occurs to me to go out and buy muffins and I bet I would if a man came to the door with some. I think this may be the answer to unemployment. Only if little girls are going to do it I think their mothers should abandon the chutney and go with them. They could canvass votes at the same time.

# November

# Glastonbury tour

I went to Glastonbury last week with my friend Charles. We wanted to see if the Tor would have a strange effect on us. Charles had a friend who was so overcome by the atmosphere halfway up that he had to turn round and come down. I felt the same way. The shallow steps are killing. Either you have to take giant strides to get one foot on each or you have to adopt a mincing gait and take several steps to a step, and once you start thinking about it you tend to fall over. There was a wind at the top which made the ears ache, and the knowledge (gleaned from a book in one of the witchcraft shops) of the death on site of the Abbot who had defied Henry VIII made one feel miserable and heavily pessimistic about the nature of humanity. Everything about Henry VIII has this effect on me. Apart from the breeze, the thought of the hanging, drawing and quartering, and the profound hope that Henry's ulcers really gave him *gyp*, I experienced little. Other people have been whisked into the air or found themselves in subterranean passages. I may have been resistant to the influences, having encountered several left-over hippies – long frocks, long hair, long whiskers, not much personal hygiene – and they always affect me like this. I find myself automatically against everything they claim to be for: love, peace, flowers, beads, beans,

everything. If you are consumed with loathing for Henry
VIII *and* contempt for the idiots in fringed waistcoats it
takes some time to remember on which moral ground you
customarily stand. I'm sure Henry and the hippies would
also have cordially detested each other. Then there were
the witches. I think I saw several – most of them running
tea-shops – but of course I could be mistaken. It's just that
witches and tea-shops seem to go together. I don't know
why and can think of no historical connection. The cream
tea is very far removed from the eye of newt and toe of
toad. Still, there is something funny about Glastonbury. I
felt that if there was some elemental force there it was

bitterly resentful of the tea-shops and was just biding its time. Something had annoyed it way back in the thirteenth century or thereabouts and it had responded with a colossal earthquake.

Going round the ruins of the abbey was at once an uplifting and even more depressing experience. What remains is still so beautiful that it is impossible to imagine the cast of mind of those who allowed it to fall into disrepair, and those who carried away chunks of it to add to their own horrid houses. Some tiny sections of tiled floor have been preserved, and the colours are so glorious that by an immense effort you can briefly visualise what the building must have been like before the hellish Henry destroyed everything. We had hired a tape describing the history and layout of the place and I was diverted to learn that each Christmas a sprig of the Glastonbury Thorn is sent to the Queen. It seemed peculiarly ironic in view of the behaviour of her predecessor. Then I thought of the other Charles – the Prince of Wales – and all was forgiven. He is quite splendidly sound on the related subjects of architecture and vandalism and would never have permitted the destruction of the abbey, or allowed those Tudor thugs to pinch bits of it.

As we approached the thorn we heard some tweeting, and there was a robin hopping about on a twig without any hint of shyness or alarm. While in fact the robin is not a very nice bird, being given to murdering his rivals or anything he sees encroaching on his territory, there is a legend that he got his red breast in trying to wrench out the thorns from the crown of Our Lord on the cross. This struck us as pleasantly symbolic and we drove home satisfied, despite not having levitated on the Tor.

# Wall to wall

We got carried away by the carpet. Not as in 'magic' – although on Thursday evening I wished we had – but more by the Stakhanovite enthusiasm of the carpet layers. 'How about this room then?' they would say, pointing eagerly at the naked boards. For a while I protested that I *liked* naked boards, but it was rather like telling the NSPCC that you didn't believe in putting warm woolies on your children. The carpet men found me incredible and/or perverse, and in the end I capitulated out of weariness; so we have carpet everywhere. Just everywhere. I'm surprised they stopped at the walls and ceiling. It feels rather like living in an inside-out bear. I begin to see why fleas congregate on furry creatures. It's easy on the feet, it's warm, silent and cosy once you get used to the idea that you're walking around on a sort of cloth – which when you come to think about it is rather unnatural and certainly sybaritic. Anyway, Alfie says it's easier to clean than boards because you just race round with the hoover. I suppose I'll get used to it.

It could have got ruined on Thursday, because the electricity went. I came home at six in the evening to find the traffic lights gone outside the zoo and at the next junction, the street lights out and most of the houses in the street in total darkness. Including ours. Everybody was trudging round with dripping candles, and no one can claim that melted wax is good for the carpet. Nor setting fire to it. The lights all went on at five the following morning, and then they all went out again for the rest of the day.

When darkness fell at about three in the afternoon I went out to catch a train somewhere and was told by the ticket man that the trains weren't really running at the moment and he didn't know how long I'd have to wait. I waited anyway. At least the lights were on in the station, so I could read the paper. I never found out what was holding the trains up, but the local explanation for the electricity failure is that somebody had dropped a firework into one of the holes (of which we now have more than road) and burnt up a cable. If a mere sparkler can bring a district to a standstill, what, I asked myself, would happen in the event of a nuclear strike?

I asked myself the same question last week when I took the daughter to a casualty ward because she had a pain in her stomach and couldn't stand up straight. There were a few staff flying about, somebody apparently breathing his last on a trolley in the corridor, and somebody else howling in agony in a curtained cubicle. Apart from them and a few people who looked as though they should be cared for in a secure environment, the place had a deserted, hopeless atmosphere. It was a Sunday morning admittedly, but no one says you can't drop a bomb on a Sunday morning.

I was reminded of a friend who worked for the council and was informed that, if hostilities should come to a head and we should indeed by subjected to a nuclear attack, he was nominated as a grave digger and should immediately take up his duties digging holes in Alexandra Park. Certainly council workers have put in a lot of practice digging holes, but we could see no reason to believe that he would be particularly spared and, good as he was at it, no reason to suppose that he could dig enough holes to accommodate a few million corpses. I suppose the simplest solution would be to leave all the existing holes in the road, and then we could all voluntarily jump in and pull them in after us. Save a lot of trouble, that would.

On the other hand, if we are to believe that Jerry Fallwell of the USA is correct, God's pets (that's him and a few of his friends) will be 'raptured' up to heaven in one piece. Perhaps I should contact him and get his advice on how to convert the carpet to the upwardly mobile type.

# Open-mouthed

Things keep surprising me. We are told to retain our childlike sense of wonder and I can't understand why. You look neither intelligent nor dignified with your mouth hanging open. It all began when I was trying to bring some order to some bookshelves and my eye fell on a work entitled *The Life of Insects* by a man with the surname Wigglesworth. It seemed so unlikely that a person with such a name would choose such a subject as his life's work. Nevertheless he clearly had – perhaps out of bravado – whereas anyone with any sense would have shortened his name to Worth and written a book about money. Then I started reading a book called *The Story of Papa's Wise Dogs* written in 1867. One of the tales concerns a Newfound-land called Lion who was given to trying to rescue people

'He went mad, poor dog'

who were trying to enjoy a quiet swim. This must have been annoying, but Lion clearly meant well and was a lovable beast; so when you get to page 65 and read at the bottom the child's query 'And what became of him at last?' you turn over with misguided twentieth-century optimism to find the words: 'He went mad, and your Uncle Harry shot him, poor dog.' Nobody really writes like that any more.

I don't know why the Victorians were considered sentimental. They strike me as quite ruthless. I have several nineteenth-century domestic encyclopaedias which contain detailed instructions on how to lay out a corpse. One minute you're reading about how to arrange the flowers for the dinner table, or how to embellish a bonnet, and the next you're into do-it-yourself morticianry. Admittedly I have one book where when you get to Childbirth you are told to turn to Parturition and when you get to Parturition you are told to go back to Childbirth, but all generations are shy about something. Every magazine you pick up these days is brimming with information about various abstruse ways of giving birth – not to mention methods of getting pregnant in the first place – but I have yet to see any recent information on what practical, immediate steps to take when Grandpapa has breathed his last. Then when I was listening to the wireless while idly dusting the bookshelves I heard an American talking about somebody who was *life-threatened*. 'Dying' is not only a more economical, but a more poetic, word. Nobody would write 'Life-threatened Egypt – I am life-threatened' and expect to get put on the stage, would they? But the Americans seem to be shyer of death than we are – and, I would have said, crazier – but I'm not sure.

I heard another programme about Orange County and the numbers of Hispanics there, giving rise to fears that

English will die out because everyone will be talking Spanish, and the man said he'd heard another man say: 'English was good enough for Jesus Christ and it's good enough for me.' Well, that was mad enough but I wasn't too smug because I watched *Black Narcissus* on the telly and there was Deborah Kerr saying of our Lord something to the effect of 'Well, he took the *shape* of a man', which is a simply walloping great heresy. Did they not have a religious advisor on that film? It's meant to be about *Anglican* nuns, but even that doesn't excuse such a blunder. My *biggest* surprise came from an Anglican nun. She wrote to me and confided that she knew dozens of women who had been raped by their fathers and who, because of this – wait for it – identified with Mary because she had been raped by God, *her* father. I'd never thought of that one and, asking around, I discovered no one else who had. Where do they dredge these ideas up? I think my correspondent may be an American Anglican nun, but that may just be wilful thinking. I am going to bed now, because I am sick of tidying up books, and if I have many more surprises my jaw will become dislocated and probably stay that way for ever.

# Strong medicine

I have packed up four large boxes of books and sent them off to the country and the shelves look hardly any different. There are still piles of books all over various floors and I still find it difficult to find one I want to read. This is probably because I only like short stories, murder stories and works on domestic economy and I've read all those already – several times. I wasted valuable minutes browsing through *Domestic Medicine* by William Buchan MD – the 17th edition published in 1800 – and learned that in cases of small-pox it is always a bad sign when the pox run into one another, and that the habit prevalent in the lower classes of keeping their children in the same linen until the disease has run its course is inadvisable. 'Cutaneous diseases are often occasioned by nastiness alone and are always increased by it.' It seems almost everyone had small-pox sooner or later in those days. And chancres and strangury and the confirmed lues and all manner of diseases too horrid for the layman to contemplate. The passions and their treatment are also included in this work – love, for instance: 'We would advise everyone, before he tampers with this passion, to consider well the probability of his being able to attain the object of his wishes' – or just read the section on virulent gonorrhoea. Fear was something else to avoid though. Apparently many women in childbirth had died of fright when they heard the parish bell tolling the death knell for some other poor lady. I think puerperal fever was the likelier cause since Buchan suggests that his fellow medical practitioners might usefully wash their hands before proceeding from patient to patient coping with the malignant, spotted or putrid fever as well as everything else. He is also contemptuous of those doctors who pride themselves on 'prognosticating, as they call it, the patient's fate, or foretelling the issue of the disease...the very embarrassment which the friends and attendants show in disguising what he has said, is generally sufficient to discover the truth' – and the patient expires of sheer

'Jesus.' Ain't never hurd _that_ word
afore in mixed cump'ny.'

terror. What with one thing and another it's a miracle anyone survived. Especially when you look at some of the remedies recommended. Still, to be fair, Buchan was mostly very sensible in his views on fresh air, cleanliness, wholesome food etc. It wasn't his fault if medicines mostly consisted of heavy metals, often dubious herbs and peculiar powders, and the common practice was to bleed, purge, vomit and poultice.

I was feeling quite poorly by the time I put Buchan aside and took up *The Animal Story Book*, a Victorian collection for children rather similar to *Papa's Wise Dogs* which I have mentioned before. There is a tale about a man taking loads of gold somewhere in his saddle bags, his little dog accompanying him. Suddenly the dog begins to exhibit signs of instability – barking and leaping and dashing back and forth, so: 'Her master was now sure that she was mad, and taking out his pistol he shot her. He rode away quickly for he loved her dearly and could not bear to see her die.' What had happened was that the stupid man had left his saddle bags under a tree and Fido was trying to tell him so. The Victorians are another good argument against the private ownership of guns. They were always shooting first and asking questions afterwards. Poor Fido.

Then I had a look at *Three Little Preachers* by Harold Murray published by the Religious Tract Society. 'Jesus? He was the God-man who loved children, wasn't he? I've seen lots of pictures of Him and He looks, oh so kind and beautiful...' That was the cottager's crippled child speaking to the kiddies of the Quality who were engaged in converting him to religion, and while everybody meant well I began to miss the rather different sentiments which characterised the earlier part of the century. I shouldn't have minded at all if somebody had shot Millie 'the wise little woman' and Teddy 'who was in one of his most thoughtful moods' and saying things like 'when we get to Heaven the poor little boys like Jackie will be the most beautiful angels'. I felt quite sick so I turned back to Buchan and learned how to make a Blistering Plaster. I don't suppose I'll ever need to but it's gratifying to know that I could if the need arose.

# December

# Skip ahoy

It was suggested recently that we should all tidy up the street outside our own front steps in order to alleviate the litter problem. The trouble with that is that many people's idea (and I do not exclude myself) of tidying up outside their own front door is to shovel the litter down to the neighbour's front door. A few weeks ago the garden was overwhelmed with black bags – I think because the refuse collectors peering round the gate came all over tired at the sight of them, and I do understand – and after a while Janet and I heaved them into the street and piled them round the bole of the lamp post. We would have put them in a nearby skip, but skips are *always* full, and always more than half full with the detritus of people other than the person who actually hired the skip in the first place. Everybody who has ever hired a skip has suffered from this problem and thus has a vengeful compulsion to put things in other people's skips. Human nature.

The reason we had so many black bags was because we'd been tidying up the house. We have thrown away a great deal but because matter can neither be created nor destroyed many things have merely been redistributed. And because of the laws of entropy many of our possessions have been rendered into dust – most of it reposing on the book-shelves. Since we find it so difficult to keep our own house in order I cannot get too annoyed with the authorities who also seem incapable of keeping things tidy. One Sunday morning I was astonished to see two people in day-glo waistcoats apparently busying themselves in the road sweeping up leaves and dog mess and old chip wrappers with dustpans and brushes. I should have thought that by now technology would have taken over and this method would have been redundant. We don't attempt to clean even the house with a dustpan and brush. We have a vacuum cleaner. Other countries send large pieces of machinery round the streets collecting up the garbage, and then go round hosing everything down. Perhaps it is impossible here because of the parked cars and the volume of moving traffic. And, of course, the holes in the road. The gas men are still going round ripping up the paving stones, old and new, and digging deep pits. It is very hard to keep things tidy when there are people burrowing everywhere – it also makes an awful lot of mud.

I was giving thanks the other day that it was too cold for bluebottles to come and infest the black bags and lay eggs in them which would turn into hordes of maggots (as happened one strike-struck summer), when I noticed a fly sitting on the kitchen table. I crept up on him and attempted to swat him with a page of manuscript, but he was too quick for me. That was several days ago and he's still around. Just one solitary fly, but enough to shame us when strangers are present and he hovers over the butter-dish. I'm determined to get him. If I can't do it by skill and dexterity with a rolled-up newspaper I shall bring down the vacuum cleaner and hoover him. I used up all the fly-spray on the plague of wasps we had earlier in the year. And one day when I ran out of fly-spray I used up a can of furniture polish. Now I come to think of it it probably made another hole in the ozone layer. I give up.

# No strings on me

Many cultures have flung up little jingles to the following effect: this is the key of the Kingdom and in that Kingdom there is a city and in that city there is a house and in that house there is a room and in that room there is a box and in that box... What this indicates to me is that most cultures have trouble tidying up. Our kingdom is a mess with new towns, motorways, collapsing sewers, conifer plantations, fields of rape, poisonous chickens, water, potatoes, etc., etc. and the hideous threat of the channel tunnel. Our cities are a more concentrated mess with litter piling up in the shopping precincts, and our house is a mess with all sorts of things.

Each room is a mess and in each room is a box – or a chest of drawers – which is also a mess. It is all very discouraging. We have somewhat sorted out the larger aspects of domestic mess; the redundant high chairs and wicker cradles have gone to the country and a no-good mattress has gone into a skip. A number of crispy shoes and my favourite coat and skirt (because the moths had got them) have been black-bagged, and some rooms look misleadingly neat. Now there are chests of drawers, cupboards, baskets, plastic carrier bags and boxes to be sorted out. In all these things are smaller boxes or bags or envelopes each containing even smaller boxes, bags and envelopes and in these are single earrings, locks of hair, keys, curtain rings, broken beads, letters, *aides-mémoire*, bills, snapshots, Deathless Thoughts on bits of paper napkin, old coins, stamps, and all manner of little articles no one knows the purpose of. These are usually *very important* things that have been put in a *safe place*: broken bits of carving from picture frames which have since been discarded because they had bits of carving missing, small hand-turned knobs from some now undiscoverable chest, a spring, some brass curtain rings and hundreds of buttons, hair pins, paper clips and perished rubber bands – all of which might *come in useful*.

There isn't any string – not even from twenty years ago – which led me to waste some time musing on the universal prevalence of sticky tape and jiffy bags. When I was an innocent child everyone saved bits of string in drawers and boxes and soup-tureens. Many cultures have played cat's cradle, but I don't suppose they do any more. Modern technology is even more impoverishing than I had thought. I found a tape measure and idly measured my fingernails. Some of them are nearly an inch long because I haven't been doing my proper housework; not real scrubbing, scouring, one-to-one-with-the-kitchen-stove type housework. Just tidying. Janet says I'm beginning unpleasantly to resemble a Chinese Mandarin who never did anything much either except for a spot of light calligraphy and watching his fingernails grow. I can't find the nail scissors. And not only is there no string any more, there aren't any spare boot-laces tucked away in a jug. The fifth son had to take the laces out of his trainers last night in order to demonstrate a trick. It was rather clever and I can't imagine how it was done.

The Fly has finally gone, which is cheering. He got even more tiresome as he grew older and colder and wearier, and while we still couldn't catch him he kept blundering into people as they sat down to supper. I got sick of explaining to strangers that he was the only one we had and I got fantastical and neurotic about him. He reminded me of a wounded tiger who takes to man-eating because everything else can run too fast. I said I was going to build a machan and tempt him out by leaving the decaying corpse of a tethered goat on the kitchen floor and smack him *wallop* when he was gorged. I began to wonder where you could get fly-paper these days and I used to hate the very sight of fly-paper. I still do but I was feeling guilty about the aerosols. Still, I shan't have to worry about flies or moths or wasps for a while. They're doubtless all wintering in corners which I have already tidied up and I won't be looking there again until several springs have passed.

# Nappy Christmas

I remember Caroline remarking once with quiet sincerity that she hadn't got a *grain* of cuddly granny in her. We were discussing the prospect of our children having children and deciding that extended holidays were *out*. Occasional formal teas, OK – but no more. Now the fourth son has come for Christmas with his baby. Well, it's actually two and mobile and talks a lot, so he isn't really a baby except that he still wears nappies and is very bossy. I did one sensible thing in my life. I ensured that any possible grandchildren should have plenty of uncles and an aunt so that now I can say firmly that I don't do any nappy-changing nor getting up in the night and mean it. He woke up the other evening and announced loudly that he wanted his daddy and doors all over the house flung open as family members shot out to reassure him. The poor child has jet lag and his sleep patterns are all to hell and it's nothing to do with me. Other people entertain him in the watches of the night. Being a grandparent is positively peaceful if you take proper precautions.

I'm going to buy him a push-chair so that everybody can take him for walks to the zoo and the park if, that is, we can negotiate our way through the traffic. For some reason whoever authorises these things has decreed that more roads need digging up before Christmas, the traffic lights are out of commission and everything is again at a standstill round here with people standing in the middle of the road directing maddened Christmas shoppers down all sorts of routes they don't want to go. The new Sainsbury's is adding to the problem since customers in motor cars have to enter from the main road which copes only with single-lane traffic and there really isn't any point in trying to go anywhere except on foot. In order to get to the pram shop we shall have to cross many dangerous roads and I'm beginning to think it's time to go to the country. This will involve different problems: streams rather than traffic, and hard slate floors which babies can hurt their knees on rather than carpets which they can spill their juice on. I had forgotten about putting things like the best china out of reach of what are usually called enquiring little fingers and keeping pan handles pointed inwards on the stove and keeping the bottoms of windows closed. Still, apart from the motor cars, it's safer in London than in the country. Now that our house is furred all over with carpet the odd tumble doesn't matter, but down there is a lot of wood and stone and open fires requiring the return of the fire guards which we lent to somebody we can't remember. I think the same person must have the cot since I know we used to have one and we haven't any more. I kept a load of baby clothes, but they're out of fashion at the moment so I think I'll keep them a bit longer for my great-grandchildren, when possibly they'll be in style again. We can't have an unfashionable baby.

Beryl has just informed me that town is unsafe for a new reason which I hadn't thought of. She spoke the other day to a rat-catcher who told her that the sewers are now so awful that the rats can't stand it so they've all come up above ground. I was vaguely planning to walk along the canal bank to the vicinity of the pram shop, thereby missing the hazardous crossings, but now I remember seeing a number of rats playing round there and I may be more alarmed by rats than by cars. Besides the baby would doubtless see them as cuddly toys and want to play with them. In the country we are seldom troubled by vermin because the place is alive with wild farm cats who present us with a different problem – the daughter tries to adopt all their kittens. The baby has just gone upstairs, followed

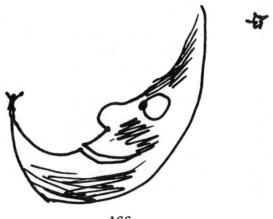

this time by Janet in a catching posture. Alfie was going to take him to the Post Office but the Post Office is on strike today. I don't know precisely why everything is so exhausting but I think *I'll* spend Christmas on the moon.

# Funny sort of flu

As I am very seldom ill (I am touching the wooden bedhead as I write) I can never understand what's happening when I begin to feel unusual. Finding that my knees will not support me, that my mind is going blank and my eyes can't see straight I imagine these symptoms are caused by the wing of the dark angel, and begin agitating myself about whether I left out anything salient in my last confession and whether I will have time to remedy the omission before either death or Christmas strikes. A few days ago, quite sure that my number was up, I began to plan a compilation of things for the family to do in my absence over Christmas and the rest of their lives when Janet staggered in with precisely the same symptoms as I was suffering from. While it is neither rational nor kind to feel pleased that somebody else is in the same plight as yourself it is nevertheless reassuring – just as long as you're pretty sure it's not the Black Death or something – and I began to feel better. Then a newsreader on the telly announced in the whimsical slot which comes at the end that there was 'ten day flu' around, and everything fell into place. I don't know why this epidemic should be considered mildly humorous but I was glad to know we were not alone.

There are, in fact, several sorts of flu around. Patrice has got one – or possibly two sorts. The first she contracted in France while staying in an *Hôtel*. She woke up one morning looking dreadful and feeling like *merde* and the proprietor with Gallic sympathy advised her that she would be much better *'chez vous, Madame'*, which is French for not wanting to be bothered with an ill English person. I remembered the old Parisian urban legend wherein an English loved-one simply disappears, bag and baggage, from his hotel room. Not only that: the hotel room disappears as well. There is no room of that number in the corridor, where the door stood there is only wall paper and perhaps a daguerreotype of the Tuileries, and the *concierge*, chambermaid, boot boy and kindly old party whom the English pair had met last night in the *salle à manger* all deny any knowledge of the missing person. The missing person has, of course, died of the plague and been spirited away in order not to discourage the hordes of tourists expected for the forthcoming *Grande Exhibition*, or whatever. I told Patrice she was quite lucky, considering. She didn't think so because when the hovercraft had conveyed her to English soil she felt so awful she hired a cab to drive her back to London and the driver insisted on making a detour to pick up his girl friend. When Patrice asked why he was doing this he said it was so that his girl friend could look after her on the journey, but when the girl friend appeared she looked even iller than Patrice, with an English flu involving coughing and sneezing. After they had gone a few miles the driver observed a cab from a rival firm plying for trade on what he considered his patch, so he stopped and leapt out to remonstrate with him. As he was doing this Patrice asked the girl friend – who was by now coughing her head off – why on earth she was coming too when she should clearly have been in bed or in hospital, and the girl said that the driver had considered Patrice's hiring him to be an excellent, economical opportunity to get the Christmas shopping done in London. This is why Patrice may now have two sorts of flu.

One sort is bad enough. I tottered into bed at 7 o'clock yesterday, incapable even of reading, but I wasn't bored because the baby refused to go to sleep and was doing the rounds of all the rooms in the house. He joined me in bed for a while together with a couple of hippopotamuses, a Garfield and a frog and we discussed the language of animals. (What *do* hippopotamuses say?) I worried for a while that he might contract my flu but then I thought that as its only notable symptoms seem to be an overwhelming urge to go to sleep and stay that way for a few days it might not be such a bad thing. May I be forgiven.

**Flamingo**

Flamingo is a quality imprint publishing both fiction and non-fiction. Below are some recent titles.

**Fiction**

☐ The Idle Hill of Summer *Julia Hamilton* £3.95
☐ Family Mashber *Der Nister* £5.95
☐ The Shadow Bride *Roy Heath* £4.95
☐ The Age of Grief *Jane Smiley* £3.95
☐ The Thirteenth House *Adam Zameenzad* £3.95
☐ Gloriana *Michael Moorcock* £4.95
☐ Sex and Sunsets *Tim Sandlin* £3.95
☐ A Kist of Sorrows *David Kerr Cameron* £3.95
☐ Home Thoughts *Tim Parks* £3.95
☐ Human Voices *Penelope Fitzgerald* £3.95
☐ Offshore *Penelope Fitzgerald* £3.95
☐ Nelly's Version *Eva Figes* £3.95
☐ The Joys of Motherhood *Buchi Emecheta* £3.95

**Non-fiction**

☐ The Dancing Wu Li Masters *Gary Zukav* £4.95
☐ The Book of Five Rings *Miyamoto Musashi* £3.95
☐ More Home Life *Alice Thomas Ellis* £3.95
☐ In the Ditch *Buchi Emecheta* £3.95

You can buy Flamingo paperbacks at your local bookshop or newsagent. Or you can order them from Fontana Paperbacks, Cash Sales Department, Box 29, Douglas, Isle of Man. Please send a cheque, postal or money order (not currency) worth the purchase price plus 22p per book (or plus 22p per book if outside the UK).

NAME (Block letters) _____

ADDRESS_____

_____

_____

# Alice Thomas Ellis

# Home Life Book Three

In this third collection of weekly articles from the *Spectator*, Alice Thomas Ellis once again brings inexhaustible wit and profound sagacity to her commentary on the ups and downs and inside-outness of daily life in town and country.

Pondering on life's little ironies as she fields minor crises from the perverse behaviour of domestic appliances to the accidents befalling Loved Ones – be they pets or people – she quips and cusses her way through the year with a mixture of *jeu d'esprit* and despair. Musing sanguinely or with a measure of hysteria on the cast of friends, family and other creatures who embroider and beleaguer her life and on matters of concern from conifers to cardboard boxes, she amuses and enlightens us as ever with those irrepressible secret-of-the-universe-type insights.

'A wonderful mixture of classical education and homespun philosophy.'                                        Robert Harris, *Observer*

'There are people who buy the *Spectator* purely to read Alice Thomas Ellis, in the same way diners willingly confront the fried eye and thorny dampness of *truite aux amandes* simply to eat the nuts off the top.'                                Clare Boylan, *Sunday Times*

**Flamingo**

**Flamingo**

Flamingo is a quality imprint publishing both fiction and non-fiction. Below are some recent titles.

**Fiction**
- ☐ In the Night Cafe *Joyce Johnson* £3.99
- ☐ Love, Bones & Water *Adam Zameenzad* £3.99
- ☐ The Vice Consul *Marguerite Duras* £3.99
- ☐ The Greenhouse *Susan Hillmore* £3.50
- ☐ Dry White Season *André Brink* £3.99
- ☐ Perfect Peace *Amos Oz* £3.99
- ☐ Night of the Weeping Women *Lawrence Naumoff* £3.99
- ☐ In Country *Bobbie Ann Mason* £3.99

**Non-fiction**
- ☐ 1791: Mozart's Last Year *H. C. Robbins Landon* £5.99
- ☐ Trivial Disputes *Fraser Harrison* £3.99
- ☐ Borrowed Time *Paul Monette* £4.50
- ☐ The Naked Civil Servant *Quentin Crisp* £3.99
- ☐ The Rites of Autumn *Dan O'Brien* £3.99

You can buy Flamingo paperbacks at your local bookshop or newsagent. Or you can order them from Fontana Paperbacks, Cash Sales Department, Box 29, Douglas, Isle of Man. Please send a cheque, postal or money order (not currency) worth the purchase price plus 22p per book (or plus 22p per book if outside the UK).

NAME (Block letters)_____

ADDRESS_____

_____

_____

While every effort is made to keep prices low, it is sometimes necessary to increase them at short notice. Fontana Paperbacks reserve the right to show new retail prices on covers which may differ from those previously advertised in the text or elsewhere.